92
EVE

C0-BJG-094

NEVER THE

Same

NEVER THE
Same

AN AUTOBIOGRAPHY

GAYLE EVERHART

BEAVERTON CHRISTIAN CHURCH
LIBRARY
13600 SW Allen Blvd.
Beaverton, OR 97005

© 2010 by Gayle Everhart. All rights reserved.

Pleasant Word (a division of WinePress Publishing, PO Box 428, Enumclaw, WA 98022) functions only as book publisher. As such, the ultimate design, content, editorial accuracy, and views expressed or implied in this work are those of the author.

No part of this publication may be reproduced, stored in a retrieval system, or transmitted in any way by any means—electronic, mechanical, photocopy, recording, or otherwise—without the prior permission of the copyright holder, except as provided by USA copyright law.

Unless otherwise noted, all Scriptures are taken from the *Holy Bible, New International Version*®, *NIV*®. Copyright © 1973, 1978, 1984 by Biblica, Inc.™ Used by permission of Zondervan. All rights reserved worldwide. WWW.ZONDERVAN.COM

Scripture references marked KJV are taken from the *King James Version* of the Bible.

Scripture references marked NASB are taken from the *New American Standard Bible*, © 1960, 1963, 1968, 1971, 1972, 1973, 1975, 1977 by The Lockman Foundation. Used by permission.

Scripture references marked NKJ are taken from the *New King James Version*, © 1979, 1980, 1982 by Thomas Nelson, Inc., Publishers. Used by permission.

ISBN 13: 978-1-4141-1418-7
ISBN 10: 1-4141-1418-4
Library of Congress Catalog Card Number: 2009902617

With gratitude to my husband for believing from the start that I could complete the following pages, and for his patience and encouragement during the process.

Introduction

ALTHOUGH FOR MANY years I sensed God's leading to pen my story, it has been with much reluctance—and certainly with no great hurry—that I have done so. I have asked myself these questions over and over: Who really cares about my story? Other than friends or family, why would anyone bother to read it? After all, I am nobody famous. I have accomplished nothing that merits notoriety.

I realize we each have a story to tell, and yet the pressing to write my own has been relentless. I began this oftentimes-tedious process many years ago; I shelved the whole venture several times. On more than one occasion I came close to deleting the manuscript from my computer and destroying the hard copy. But I found myself unable to do so.

Along with my desire to be obedient to my Lord, I completed this writing in honor of my son Eric, who deserved so much more. If I could "undo" but one choice in my lifetime, I would "undo" that choice I made so many years ago—the one after which I have never been the same.

In everything that has come my way—some admittedly self-imposed—it has been Jesus Christ who has consistently provided me with strength and hope, along with the awareness that He always works for good, even when it is difficult to see any good.

What I find most remarkable is that, in spite of me and in spite of circumstances beyond my control, God has chosen to use my life for His good purpose. By His incredible grace alone, I have penned the following pages. I pray that through my story hearts will be touched for the sweet babies and for women facing an unwanted pregnancy or the aftermath of abortion. I pray consciences will be stirred to ask, "What can I do?" God's Word states we will be held accountable for what we knew.

I pray that you will be encouraged to hold on, in faith, to whatever calling or promise God has for you. More importantly, that you will be obedient to that calling, wherever it may lead, knowing with absolute certainty that God had a plan and a purpose for you long before you were conceived in your mother's womb.

> "Your eyes saw my unformed body, all the days ordained for me were written in your book before one of them came to be."
>
> —Psalm 139:16

Chapter One

IT'S REALLY NO big deal. You'll be okay," assured the sincere-looking woman sitting at the receptionist's desk. My eyes probed hers in a desperate attempt to draw comfort and truth from the confidence she exuded. I had no clue then what a big deal this otherwise ordinary Tuesday morning would prove to be. Or that it would not be long before I would not be "okay" at all. I had no clue then how profoundly that one choice would forever change me.

I was raised in a Christian home. I grew up going to church every Sunday and to services and events during the week. I gave my heart to Jesus at an early age.

And as a teenager, I had an abortion.

Sadly, the church is not immune. Statistics show that Christian girls from Christian homes are having abortions as often as non-Christians. Women who have had abortions sit beside us in the pews, lead us in worship, and serve God faithfully in many ways.

I know several Christian women, outside of my work with the Pregnancy Resource Centers, who have divulged to me their deepest secret, their deepest heartache. Each greatly regrets the choice she once made to have an abortion. Each has chosen to keep that choice and the resulting pain a secret. It is not something most people really want to think or talk about. Not even the church.

I was eighteen years old at the time of my abortion, and abortion had only been legal in the United States for three years. I remember well the controversy and the debates leading up to the landmark date of the legalization of abortion. I had engaged in heartfelt debates with my friends, where I consistently stood for life, regardless of the circumstance. A life is a life—created in the image of God—I insisted. In my heart, I understood the value of life.

Yet when I found myself unwed and pregnant, I panicked. My thoughts on abortion, which were once so easy to sort through, suddenly became a muddled mess. Although I still believed that abortion was wrong, the thought of my parents learning I had been sexually active was unbearable. Any inner strength I thought I possessed vanished.

Over a span of sixteen years after my abortion, God spoke to me through two different people, telling me that one day He would be using me in a ministry for grieving women. Today He is doing so in a way I never imagined—by giving me the immense privilege of introducing abortion-vulnerable women to their babies on the ultrasound screen. Time and time again I witness hearts softened, as mamas realize their baby is just that—a baby, and not merely an inconvenient blob of tissue.

I tell these women that I understand what they are going through, that I have "been there." I tell them that while I know firsthand how scary and hard it all can be, I also know how destructive and painful the choice of abortion can be.

I saw Olivia for an ultrasound. Olivia had aborted her pregnancy one year earlier. Now she was pregnant again and planning another abortion. When I shared my story with her, her eyes filled with tears.

"You are the first who has understood," Olivia said. "Everyone else tells me I made the best choice, that I need to forget about it. You are the first who has understood my pain. I figured since I've already had an abortion, I'm going to hell anyway, so what difference will one more make? There's no hope for someone like me. I mean, what kind of person kills her own baby? It just hurts so badly. Can you please help me?"

"No, I cannot," I told her. "But I can tell you about someone who can. His name is Jesus, and He is the One who has helped me."

Olivia gave her heart to Jesus that afternoon and left her ultrasound appointment excited about the life she was carrying. Several months later, I experienced the remarkable blessing of holding her precious baby boy in my arms.

Olivia's story is not unique. Most of these women just need someone to listen, someone to understand. They need to be told the truth in love. Olivia's story is the first of many that are intertwined throughout the following pages. Out of respect for the privacy of these women, I have changed their names.

From the time I was a young girl, I sensed God's call on my life. One Sunday morning when I was six years old, I felt a tug on my heart when the pastor gave the altar call. Hand in hand, my dad and I walked down the aisle as the congregation sang "Just As I Am." On a Sunday evening

soon afterwards, I was baptized. As I was lifted up out of
the baptismal water, God impressed upon my heart that He
was setting me apart for a particular work. For a long time I
supposed this meant the mission field, perhaps overseas.

What I find incredibly humbling is that, in spite of
everything, God has been faithful. He has brought His plans
for my life to fruition.

Chapter Two

FROM THE OUTSIDE, my childhood appeared ideal. I received piano and art lessons, along with a private, Christian education. Many days were spent bicycling and scooter riding, licking melting popsicles, nibbling on sugar-coated strawberries, and splashing in our built-in swimming pool in Southern California.

We had numerous pets: rabbits, horses, goats, chickens, and dogs. My favorites were Snowball, a beautiful white rabbit, and Trudy, a fat, black, short-legged dog. One day, Snowball died. I can still remember the ache in my heart. Some said that Trudy looked like a hairy pig. She really was ugly, but I loved her just the same. The night she died was one of the longest of my young life. I slept on the floor at her side until her breathing stopped.

I spent a lot of time playing dolls, house, and store, as well as hosting lemonade stands. I shared those carefree days mainly with my neighbor-friend, Lillie, with whom I am blessed to still be friends with today. Often, our two sisters joined us.

One of our favorite pastimes was talking about "growing up." We meticulously described our futures, as if we had them all figured out. We never considered our futures would be anything but perfect. With precise detail, we depicted what our houses would look like, the items (in exact amounts) that we would find in our refrigerators and cupboards at any given time, the flowers in our yards, and even the names and ages of our children. As silly as this may sound, there was a sweet innocence to it. The future promised nothing but grandeur.

I enjoyed our many family camping trips. What I treasured most about these times were the rare moments of solitude, sitting, and pondering, overcome by God's incredible creation. These times of communion between my Lord and me were like no other. They were also fleeting times because, invariably, the call of my parents, the squeals of my siblings, or some other unwelcome distraction would abruptly jar me back to a world that seemed mundane in comparison.

But then there were marshmallows to roast and songs to sing around the campfire. Gazing into the glow of the warm and colorful dancing flames, my thoughts would once again drift away to some distant place.

From early on, I loved to write. Clutching a spiral notebook about, I paused during moments of "inspiration" to jot down my thoughts and story ideas. I frequently curled up in my dad's comfy, overstuffed chair with paper and pen, absorbed in my own little world, as the clamor of household activity went on around me.

One Mother's Day when I was twelve years old, I presented my mom with a collection of my writings, along with idyllic scenes I had clipped from magazines. Noted below each scene were "profound words of wisdom" concerning womanhood and mothering. What did I know of such things? How my mom must have inwardly smiled at my childhood naivety.

Seeking solitude in which to pen my deepest thoughts, I often climbed the thick trunk of the massive walnut tree in our front yard and across its wide limbs, onto the roof of our home. Thus perched, I surveyed below and all around in search of writing material. Although I sat in plain view, I was allowed these times without question. I do not recall ever being bothered while up there on that roof.

Those were the good times, the privileged times.

There were times that were not as good. Although there are circumstances in my life I would change if I could, I have come to realize that in one way or another, each has brought me good. I have learned to trust God and rely on His strength rather than on my own which, at its best, is frail.

Until my seventh birthday, my life remained fairly unmarred. Shortly afterwards, however, my innocence was shattered. While I sat on my uncle's lap one evening watching a home movie, he fondled me. My parents were sitting nearby, oblivious. The others in the room—including my uncle's wife—were also oblivious to what was occurring. This was an entirely unfamiliar experience for me; I had no idea what to make of it.

The morning following that first incidence of sexual abuse, I sat at the breakfast table, watching my mom scurry around with her usual morning activities. After a time of quiet contemplation, I asked my mom why my uncle had touched me in that way. I asked this question as if it were an ordinary occurrence.

My mom became quiet. Color drained from her face.

My dad, who had been outside tending to our many animals, entered the back door. My mom asked me to repeat my question. When Dad heard it, his face turned ashen. From my parents' somber responses, I learned this was the gravest of matters. *Nothing* about it was ordinary.

Looking back, I am grateful for how my parents responded. Never once did they question the validity of what I was telling them. Never was I made to feel any blame. There was never the slightest hint I might be imagining or exaggerating anything. They made it plain to me that what my uncle had done was wrong, and that he alone was at fault.

This uncle, who was my dad's sister's husband, was not the norm in our family. My dad and both of his brothers are godly men of the highest integrity. My grandfathers were the same.

Soon after learning of my sexual abuse, my dad confronted my uncle at his workplace. Fearful of reacting in a way he might regret later, Dad had asked an associate pastor from our church to accompany him. My uncle vowed—with the pastor as witness—that he would never again behave toward me in such a manner. Many years passed before my parents learned that on numerous other occasions through the years, my uncle had not kept his word to my dad. Although my parents had clearly told me when I first told them of my sexual abuse that it was not my fault, still I felt shame; as if somehow I had taken part. I was too humiliated to tell my parents after that first time. Due to the naiveté of childhood, I was not able to fully grasp what was occurring during those times my uncle took from me what was not his to take. Not all of his inappropriate actions towards me were physical. Some were overt sexual innuendos. Not until I was older and had gained an adult understanding of such things, did I begin to look back with clarity and a sickening awareness.

Around the time my uncle first violated me, I changed from a chatty, outgoing little girl into a painfully awkward and shy little girl. I became uncomfortable with myself and the stranger I had become. It was as if I had lost "me." For a long time I stayed walled up inside my own hurt—lost, confused, and feeling completely out of place. Inside I was broken, but nobody realized it. My self-confidence spiraled down into a slippery pit that would take me years to clamber out of.

Concerned by my social clumsiness, my mom insisted I join in with school and church groups, coaching me to "just be friendly."

If only it had been that simple! I watched the other girls. They appeared to possess such poise, always having the perfect thing to say. As much as I wanted to, I never possessed such poise.

Due to my lack of any natural athletic ability or probably—more accurately—due to zero self-confidence, I was always the last one picked when teams were chosen. "You get Gayle. There's no one left to pick," one relieved team captain would announce to the other. How awful those times felt, knowing one unlucky team had gotten stuck with me.

During my sixth-grade year, each student was required to recite a poem from memory. I rehearsed mine over and over until I at last felt confident. The big day arrived. Due to dread, I had scarcely slept the night before, praying intently for time to miraculously skip a day. But the next day came anyway. I lay there in bed, with the morning sun peeping through the edge of the window shade, and realized there was no escape. I felt ill.

Later that morning, as another student eloquently delivered her presentation, my stomach churned. Knowing my turn was next, my thoughts tangled and my heart pounded.

Then it was my turn.

"We can't hear you," announced the school principal. She was substituting for the regular teacher that day. "Start over and speak up," she ordered.

With my heart racing and my pores sweating, I went back to the beginning.

"We still can't hear you. Speak up."

Shamed beyond belief, my voice weakened with each try. Hot tears stung my eyes, fogging my glasses. Laughter erupted from my classmates. I don't remember how many times this scene repeated itself. At the time, it felt like forever.

It was at such times that God whispered to my soul, assuring me of His love, reconfirming that He had set me apart for a particular work. This reassurance from my Savior fueled and encouraged me. The awareness of His presence was at times so consuming, I would have to stop, momentarily incapable of focusing on anything else. It was at the times I hurt the most that God held me the closest, lifting me far above my loneliness and pain.

One pleasant occurrence during my sixth-grade year came the morning a missionary woman spoke to our class. I do not recall her name, or even her face. However, her passion in regards to her work with orphans at the Mukti Mission in India and the stirrings evoked within me, I *do* recall. Later that afternoon I excitedly replayed all to my mom, who purchased a book about the mission. Turning the pages over and over again, I was utterly captivated with every word and picture.

"For our next family vacation can we go to India? Maybe we will find some orphans we can bring home with us," I pleaded with my mom.

I thought about the Mukti Mission for a long time to come, and wondered if this was where God would one day be using me.

Lillie and I, and often our two sisters, played "orphanage," scattering unclothed baby dolls around my family's backyard. We pretended to happen across one as we strolled along. With great flair and dramatization, we scooped these poor, helpless "orphans" into our arms and rushed back to the "orphanage" to wash, doctor, clothe, and feed them.

I repeatedly asked God, "Please leave a baby on our front porch," imagining a scene of waking one morning to a baby's cry and flinging open the front door to discover an abandoned baby, who would become my permanent charge.

With the distractions of life, these imaginings eventually waned. One distraction in particular made everything else—at least for a while—not matter at all. It was one of my saddest days ever. It was the day my Grandma Grace died from cancer. She was gentle and kind and always had time to sit with me. Watching my grandfather crying was sadder still.

The day Grandma died, I felt as though part of me died too. I was appalled that the rest of the world went on as usual, as if nothing had happened. Didn't everyone realize Grandma had just died? For a time, I wondered if God had abandoned me and the whole world. Why would He take Grandma away? I questioned Him directly, asking if He still cared. And yet even through this He loved me, and He gave us all a wonderful gift.

God first gave this gift to my dad, who in turn shared it with us. My dad had lost his own mother to cancer when he was a young boy. He had always shared a special bond with his mother-in-law, my Grandma Grace. Shortly after Grandma's death, as my dad was walking down the hospital steps to leave for home, he heard the sound of beautiful music coming from the heavens. This brought immense comfort to him and to me.

Life moved on, but for me life was hard. There was nowhere I felt as though I entirely fit in. Feelings of awkwardness and uncertainty were commonplace. Although I am the firstborn of five, and our home bustled with the exuberance of a large family, friends, and pets, I felt alone.

I spent a lot of time trying to figure God out. I lay awake many nights, striving to get to the bottom of things, asking God this and that, and why and how. God's creation and His attributes both fascinated and disturbed me. I wanted to make sense of it all. After a long period of fitful wrestling, I would at last arrive at a place of simply trusting. Of simply resting in the fact that He is God and I am not, and finally coming to realize that if I were to fully comprehend, then God would not truly be God, omnipotent and above all else.

Today I am thankful for—and see the benefit of—these times of wrestling with God, as a hunger for God and His Word was swelling up inside me, until nothing less would suffice. I came to recognize once and for all that Jesus is—without exception—the singular answer to all my questions.

Chapter Three

A S TIME PROGRESSED, my energies turned from rescuing abandoned babies and other childhood pastimes and focused on my teenage years, where I discovered a whole new world—a world that would prove to be a struggle all the way through. While I desired to remain separate from the secular world about me, I fit in so much easier there. I found the "world" far more comfortable than the constraints and unspoken rules of the Christian world I knew. The church girls appeared to "have it all together," or so it seemed to me at the time. The youth group "cliques" were not easy to join. It seemed that it took a "secret code" or a certain "look" to be a part.

When the time came for me to enter junior high school, my parents offered me the option of continuing with Christian school or venturing into the public-school arena. I chose to give public school a try. My new circle of friends consisted of non-Christians. As a result, my mindset and choices often reflected the influence of associating myself with the world, as opposed to the things of Christ. I regularly teetered dangerously in the middle, often tilting too far in the wrong direction.

While worldly attractions loomed large, I also experienced a sense of disdain. I knew those attractions were in direct opposition to the God I loved. Yet the battle raged within.

When I entered high school, I was elated to discover that the boys had grown taller—*much* taller. I no longer towered over them. Although I always had a crush on one boy or another, God was faithful in this too, so often protecting me from my own foolish self.

As a teenager I was particularly aware of God's shielding during the opportunities to do drugs. Most of my friends indulged. I never could. There was always that still, small voice holding me back. This was an area where He gave no slack.

There were other areas where God loosened the reins, and I did cross the boundaries He had set. However, even in these I was keenly aware of His ongoing attempts to draw me back to the safety of His statutes.

My heavenly Father often used my earthly father to rein me in. No matter what I did, my dad *always* found out. My mom used to tell me she had two eyes in the back of her head. I was never convinced of this, but I was sure Dad had at least that many in the back of *his* head.

For instance, at one point I tried my hand at writing romance. Although I knew very little about such things, I penned steamy pages and then ashamedly crumpled them up and flushed them down the toilet. I was sure I would have died from utter shame if anyone ever read the sultry words I had written. Well, Dad came across my work when he unclogged the paper-logged toilet. He hollered at me to come into the bathroom then stood in front of me, holding a dripping wet, soggy paper. He read a couple of sentences out loud and demanded an explanation. My hot face must have been redder than the reddest apple. I was absolutely tongue-tied. How could I possibly explain this away?

The following incident was more serious. For some unfathomable reason, my friend Cathy and I decided to give shoplifting a try. On several occasions, we slipped items into our purses or under our jackets without paying for them. One afternoon this came to an end. Cathy and I were just about to get onto our bikes to flee, when out of the corner of my eye, I saw a chubby man in a white dress shirt, running through the store and out the door.

"Stop, you two!" he ordered.

I froze, sick with fear. My friend snickered as she took a step to get on her bicycle. The man told her she'd best stand still. He then instructed us to re-enter the store and directed us up a flight of stairs, where we were shown into a small room and told to sit down. A police officer soon arrived and telephoned our parents. Before long, I heard the sound of footsteps through the closed door and the voice of my friend's dad:

"Well, neighbor, it looks like we have a couple of criminals on our hands." He chuckled.

The door opened, and our fathers entered. My friend's dad had a spark of humor in his eyes as he patted my dad on the back. My dad's eyes, however, were filled with tears. He looked at me with the most pained expression I had ever seen on his face. The police officer described at length how serious the punishment could be, and then we were released to go home with our dads. He also warned us that if there should be a next time, we would be arrested and charged.

In the store parking lot, my dad silently tossed my bicycle into the bed of his pickup truck. The drive home was not very long, but it felt like an eternity. I don't remember my dad saying a word. He didn't have to. I knew without question that I had broken his heart.

Once home, I watched my bicycle being raised to the rafters of the garage. Dad informed me I would not be riding my bike for the next six months. Mom met us at the front door, her face puckered in a look of disapproval. All I felt was disgrace. No real punishment was necessary. Knowing I had truly grieved my dad was enough of a consequence for me.

I loved the Lord and did not want to grieve Him, either, but I struggled between my desire to please Him and the draws of the world around me. I dabbled in areas I never should have dabbled. During these times of rebellion I was not happy sinning and I sensed the Holy Spirit's conviction. For me, there was no peace in abiding outside of Him.

I transferred to a different high school following my sophomore year, desiring to make a break from the acquaintances I had entangled myself with. However, I still did not associate with other Christians, nor was I at ease participating in the activities of non-Christians. I did not feel comfortable in either world and ended up with not many friends for quite some time.

Chapter Four

DURING MY JUNIOR year of high school I worked as a counter girl for a popular restaurant. I enjoyed the added income, which far exceeded my allowance. The only jobs I had held up to this point were babysitting and helping out at my dad's transmission business.

I worked at this restaurant for about one year, until my parents insisted I resign, due to my declining school grades. At the close of my final shift, Jerry, the night manager who I thought was cute and had a nice smile, asked if I would like to go out some time.

I had dated very little before this, and I had never had a serious boyfriend. The closest I came before Jerry was Peter. I really did care for Peter, but he broke off our relationship when he learned I was not willing to sleep with him. A couple of other possibilities never made it beyond the first date or two. My interest typically waned when I discovered these knights in shining armor were less than gallant.

One frustrated suitor had told me, "If you're waiting for Mr. Right, forget it. There is no such thing." Well, *he* certainly wasn't Mr. Right. I later learned he was married and quite the Romeo.

Jerry, on the other hand, was a gentleman. I never felt pressured to sleep with him. He was several years older than I and—contrary to Peter, who had no job and no car—Jerry had a decent job and a cool car. My mom, however, was skeptical about Jerry's car. It was a popular sports model, advertised as the "Sexy European Car."

My parents were concerned that Jerry did not at that time know Jesus. However, my own relationship with Jesus was far from where it should have been. For me, it really was not all that important where Jerry stood with the Lord. Sadly, God was not part of any aspect of our relationship. As time passed, we grew more and more comfortable with one another.

Then, on one unforgettable and life-transforming afternoon, I discovered to my despair that I was pregnant.

I was petrified of going to my family doctor for a pregnancy test. I knew my parents would be sent the bill. So I regrettably turned to Planned Parenthood, who advertised confidential pregnancy tests.

"I have to have an abortion," I blurted out to Jerry in the parking lot of Planned Parenthood, following my positive pregnancy test result. Jerry did not respond one way or another, making it that much easier for me to go through with my plan. How tragic that neither of us gave a decision of such immense implications more time or consideration! How sad that we did not see that what we considered a bothersome inconvenience was really our baby!

If only I had known then all that would ensue. If only I had taken a little more time—just a *little* more time.

Maybe I would have made a decision based on careful thought and prayer rather than solely on fear. Maybe my baby's life would have been spared and my heart spared the agony that followed, which would haunt me for years to come.

The thought of my parents learning I was pregnant was my biggest fear and the prevalent factor playing into my decision. I did not want them to know I had been sexually active. I did not want to cause them hurt or shame, especially my dad. I have been blessed with a wonderful dad. From the start, his acceptance and love for me has been without conditions. He has always loved me just for being *me*.

How would our church react? How would my strict Baptist (and oftentimes legalistic) extended family react? Would they accept this child, or would he or she forever be labeled as illegitimate? I am the oldest of my siblings and the oldest of my cousins. As far as I knew *then*, this was a first for my family. I was absolutely terrified.

I briefly considered adoption, but quickly dismissed this option from my mind. I couldn't imagine carrying a baby for nine months just to give it away. My baby would think his mama didn't want or love him. The thought of this made me heartsick. Besides, my parents and everybody else would know I was pregnant. They would all know I had been having sex! It was not that I did not want my baby; it was just from my blurred perspective a lousy time to be pregnant.

I realize that for many, the concept that a woman could not give her baby away, but she could have her baby aborted, is completely illogical. I can understand this distorted form of rationalization only because I have been there. I know how powerful and destructive self-preservation can be. And I certainly know how skewed a person's decision-making abilities can be at such an emotionally overwhelming time. I reasoned with myself that with abortion, my baby would at least be in heaven; with adoption I would have no control over my baby's future. Open adoptions were not common back then as they are today.

I am not attempting to justify anything. My decision to abort my baby was extremely selfish of me and very wrong. I am only trying to bring some understanding and hopefully compassion into how a woman might be processing through such a choice as this.

I have heard it said that if a woman is truly a Christian—or if she truly believes abortion is wrong—she would never have an abortion. I know neither is true. My walk with Christ at the time was extremely weak, but I was still a Christian. I truly believed abortion was wrong. Yet I had an abortion.

Again, statistics show that Christians are having as many abortions as non-Christians. I strongly believe this is an area in which the church needs to step in and become more vocal. This is a matter of life and death.

I also need to clarify that I do not believe that placing a baby for adoption is giving that baby away. I believe that by and large, this decision is based on a selfless love on the birth mother's part for her baby and demonstrates tremendous strength of character. I have the utmost respect for women who choose adoption. If only I had had such strength! I can only begin to imagine how difficult it would be to make and then follow through with this choice.

I counsel the clients I see at the Pregnancy Resource Centers that none of their choices are easy. Parenting is not easy, the choice of adoption cannot possibly be easy, and I certainly know abortion is not easy. I encourage these young women not to make what seems like the *easy* choice, but rather the one she knows in her heart is the *right* choice—a choice she must live with for the rest of her life. If she expresses a belief in God, I ask her how she believes God views abortion. I then encourage her to make a choice which honors Him.

I look back with regret that I did not seek godly counsel at this point of crisis in my life. I could have gone to a pastor or youth-group leader at our church, my aunt, or—now I know—my parents. Instead, I chose to look to non-Christians for help with my dilemma. Those who I felt were safe.

I did confide in my sister, who took it very nonchalantly. But she was only fifteen, and legalized abortion was still new. I am sure she did not fully understand the significance of the matter. I wonder now if I confided in her as a cry for help. Perhaps I hoped the news would escape her and reach the ears of my parents, who would have stopped me from going through with my abortion.

I rationalized my decision to abort my baby in an attempt to *ease* the guilt of that choice. Abortion would be a quick and easy fix. Nobody would ever have to know. Abortion would put my inopportune dilemma behind me. I *knew* I was sinning, but it would be okay, I consoled myself. God would forgive me. I would make it up to Him later. I tried to persuade myself that it would truly be that simple. I did not realize at the time that it would become much more complex than that.

For too long my outlook on sin had been far too casual. I did not adequately perceive the gravity of sin or the immense cost of the shed blood of my merciful Savior. And for me, the abortion proved to be tremendously costly. It would take a very long time to heal.

Planned Parenthood made it *way* too easy. Just sign on the dotted line and pay the $200 fee (today it is substantially higher). They may have provided me with pre-abortion counsel, but I honestly don't remember any. I have no memory of being told about the possible emotional and physical risks related to abortion. No one presented information regarding fetal development. No one at Planned Parenthood counseled me that I might regret my decision. The subject of adoption was never broached.

I don't recall being encouraged to give my decision careful thought—to be certain the decision I was making was true to my heart and religious beliefs rather than one centered on fear. I was eighteen years old at the time of my abortion and would have to live with that decision for the rest of my life. I don't recall Planned Parenthood suggesting I tell my parents, or anyone else for that matter, that I was pregnant, let alone considering an abortion.

Today I honestly believe that if I had been given different counsel, counsel which honored life, I would not have gone through with the abortion. If I had sat with a counselor who would have taken the time to remind me of my core beliefs, who would have cared enough to speak the truth, I am confident the outcome would have been different. I needed to know I was not alone, that someone would walk me through this. I needed to hear that abortion could easily turn a bad situation worse, rather than make it better. I needed someone to help me see my baby as a blessing rather than a bother.

Although I made the final choice, I resent the lack of counsel I received. The only session I took part in at Planned Parenthood was a group setting focusing on the financial aspect of paying for the abortion procedure. I felt a bit smug that I was the only one who would be paying cash. The others would be covered by state assistance.

Ironically, the fact that I paid cash for my baby's death would trouble me for years to come. Essentially, I had hired

Planned Parenthood as the "hit man" to do away with my unwanted child. This would prove to be an enormously heavy burden to bear and the largest emotional hurdle of all.

The morning of the abortion of my baby, the hospital room felt chilly and harsh. A nurse bustled about, calling out names from a clipboard. I lay numbly on a gurney, staring blankly at the ceiling, awaiting my turn.

A doctor with dark brown eyes, a dark beard, and wearing green scrubs wheeled me off. He sported a twinkle in his eyes and made lighthearted small talk. I took great offense at his light and jovial demeanor. My state of mind was anything but light.

I cannot say that my recollection of my experience with Planned Parenthood is totally accurate, but this is how my mind remembers that day—the day of the snuffing away of the life of my son, the life which had barely begun and which was deprived of experiencing all that God had purposed for him …

When I awoke from the abortion procedure, I found myself in what seemed to be a dark, dismal pit. "Dear God, what have I done?" I whispered.

A heavy and suffocating sadness engulfed me. I wanted to vomit. With every ounce of my being I knew exactly what I had done and it felt so despicable.

Once the nurse determined me to be "medically" stable, she discharged me. She never asked me how I was doing otherwise. I was escorted by way of wheelchair out of a side door of the hospital, across the asphalt, and through the back entrance of the Planned Parenthood clinic, where my ride—a friend—awaited. The creaking of the wheels turning accompanied by the sound of the hospital attendant's cheerful whistle aided in creating an eerie and surreal mood. I stared straight ahead, my hands folded neatly in my lap. The only thought running through my mind was, *How can he whistle?* Even today, I can almost hear that whistle.

I waited at my friend's house until Jerry picked me up later that evening after he got off work. I had slept over at another friend's house the night before, so my parents would have no suspicions. They had no idea what their daughter had undergone that day.

As the hours passed into early evening, the heaviness seemed to lift. The sun slid beyond the horizon, and my mood elevated. I experienced a sudden sense of liberation. Breathing a deep sigh of relief, I swooped across the lawn and driveway, with my arms flapping like bird's wings, as Jerry arrived at my friend's house to pick me up.

I'm free. My inconvenience is now a thing of the past, I lied to myself.

Life went on as it does. I busied myself with finishing up the medical assisting course I was taking. A pang of guilt stung when I lied to my classmates and teacher that I had been sick at home the day before.

"But I'm fine now," I said assertively, in a meager attempt to convince myself that I was truly okay.

Wedding preparations were also underway. The ceremony was planned for six weeks following the abortion. Later, this would also cause remorse. I could have gone through with the pregnancy. Jerry and I had already set a wedding date. But then my parents (and everybody else) would have known I was not a virgin when I strolled down that aisle, dressed all in white.

With the weight of completing school, putting the wedding together, and the emotional aftermath of the abortion, I became a nervous wreck. I would glance down and see my hands trembling. Sleep eluded me. At times I battled with an almost overpowering urge to bring physical harm—even death—to myself. I longed to run far away and hide someplace where no one could ever find me. Bouts of panic attacked, particularly at night.

Due to my anxious state, my mom scheduled an appointment for me with our family physician. He diagnosed me as being under enormous stress due to the pressures of completing school and getting married. "You're awfully young, you know."

I didn't respond. I also didn't tell him about the abortion. He prescribed the tranquilizer, Valium. They thoroughly knocked me out. One afternoon, my piano instructor came to our home to bring me a wedding gift. My mom was unable to stir me from a deep sleep. One evening, I groggily found my way home after babysitting for the neighbor children. Their mom had had difficulty waking me from the sofa. I hated how the tranquilizers made me feel, and my lack of control while under their effect. After taking perhaps three or four doses, I flushed the remainder of the pills down the toilet.

Years later, I tearfully told my mom about the abortion. Her response was one of hurt that I had not felt as though I could come to her or Dad, and that they had been left so totally in the dark. Years after that, my heart beat vigorously against my chest, and my voice quivered, as I told my dad about the biggest regret of my life.

"Well you know that God loves you and has forgiven you, right? And you know that I love you, too?"

"Yes, Dad, I do."

If I had only found the courage to face my parents with the truth, I would have found the strength to go through with my pregnancy. My parents would have been there for me and would have helped me through.

Chapter Five

LOOKING BACK, I do not understand the rush to get married. I was so young. Jerry was young. I was not pregnant when we became engaged. I just loved the whole romantic aspect of it all: planning a wedding, picking out the dress, wearing a veil, envisioning friends and family gleefully opening the wedding announcement and weeping with joy as I walked down the aisle.

Painted on the canvas of my mind was a blissful picture of married life, with pies baking in the oven and me puttering about, cheerfully doing laundry and other household duties. I am baffled now why I imagined it to be so intriguing. When I lived at home, I avoided laundry and other household tasks like the plague. All the same, I pictured these activities in the setting of marriage as something marvelous. I also looked forward to living out from under my parents' roof and saw only the "happily ever after."

To some extent I felt obligated to marry Jerry, as if getting married would somehow make everything right with God and alleviate my guilt: the guilt I felt for having sex outside of marriage, and later on the added guilt I felt for having aborted our baby.

The wedding ceremony went as planned in a pretty, stained-glass-windowed church on the eve of Easter Sunday. While Easter represents joyous new life, our marriage, on the other hand, would not be as joyous.

From the beginning, our marriage was not as I had dreamed. Neither Jerry nor I was at a place in our lives conducive for such a union. There was very little communication between us, and any spiritual connection was nonexistent. The abortion of our baby only complicated things. On a rare occasion I would bring up the abortion to Jerry, but we never talked about it. The subject was always squelched, while inside, I was torn to shreds. Jerry told me I needed to put the abortion behind me. It was over. I tried heeding his advice, but I was incapable of moving on.

Shortly after our wedding, I began experiencing terrifying nightmares wherein I visualized my aborted baby boy in hell, his arms and legs flailing, his little cry piercing my soul. I would reach out to him, wanting so badly to gather him into my arms, but I was never able to reach far enough. I would awake paralyzed, incapable of making even the slightest shift of a muscle, my skin soaked, my pulse pounding.

One evening, I wept aloud while watching a television movie about an unwed, pregnant teenager who courageously chose to give her baby life and raise the child in spite of the obstacles. I knew a single young woman through a friend of our family, who faced the music and had her baby. I beat myself up inside. *Why couldn't I have been that brave?*

I felt so alone. Only Jerry and a couple of others knew about the abortion. Jerry did not see any benefit in talking about that which was over and done with. The others could not connect with what I was going through. To them it seemed like my abortion was no big deal.

I agreed I needed to move on, but I also knew that what I had done really *was* a big deal. I needed to fully confront the abortion before I would ever know true healing. I had no idea how to begin that process, however, and I didn't know if I could handle everything that would ensue if I did. So for a long time I suppressed the memories, the sadness, and the pain as best I could.

The one place I had no control was in my dreams. Sleep had become my enemy. I dreaded falling asleep. I never knew whether those hours would bring torture or welcome slumber. Though often exhausted from a fitful sleep the night before, I resisted closing my eyes, crying out to God, "Please, just tonight, let me sleep in peace."

I had repented to God regarding my abortion, but I could not accept His forgiveness. My heart never questioned His love or ability to forgive; I just felt so undeserving. Forgiving myself was beyond my capacity to do.

After about two years of marriage, I again was pregnant. One horrifying evening, Jerry rushed me to the hospital emergency room. It appeared that I was bleeding to death. The attending physician was kind and sensitive. He explained that I was miscarrying. Although I knew better, a part of me wondered if God was punishing me for my abortion. Secretly, I feared I would never be allowed to have children, that I would forever pay the price for that one dreadful act.

The emotional aftereffects of the miscarriage were less severe than with the abortion, but it was still difficult. I had now experienced the loss of two babies, and at times the pain was overwhelming.

On Mother's Day, a little over one year following my miscarriage, I gave birth to a precious baby boy. I knew my son's birth this specific day had not occurred by chance. I saw it as a manifestation of God's gracious love and wondrous mercy. I relished my new role as a mother. Never before had I known such an all-encompassing love for another human being.

I was blessed with the privilege of being a stay-at-home mom. Jerry worked many long, hard hours to provide for his family. Seventeen months following the birth of our son, and after a grueling labor, I gave birth to our dear daughter. I now felt doubly blessed.

Chapter Six

MY PARENTS AND siblings moved from California to Oregon shortly before the birth of my son. We remained close, considering the miles between us. Jerry's family, as well as some of my own, still lived nearby. We were gifted with wonderful neighbors and a few good friends.

On the outside I appeared happy, and in some ways, I was. However, in some extremely crucial ways, life was discouraging and hard. Our marriage was not good. Our family life was not what I longed for. I struggled with anger toward my husband and even, at times, toward God for allowing things to be as they were. I realize it would be far more telling if I went into further detail here. I have gone back and forth in my mind about this—I have prayed about it, and out of love for my husband, I have decided not to. I will say that life with my husband was not, back then, as it should have been for our children or for me. I allowed resentment to take root and fester in my heart. This bitterness, in turn, trickled out all over the place.

In addition, there was a heaviness I repeatedly attempted to stifle and shove deep inside, where nobody could detect the truth. I still deeply regretted the abortion of my first pregnancy. For me, abortion had not been the quick and easy fix I had intended. A misguided belief has imbedded itself in the minds of so many: that abortion is a simple remedy, a Band-Aid, or "no big deal." So many hearts have been hardened to the truth.

I believed from early on that my aborted baby was a boy, and I named him Eric. Today, since finding full healing in Jesus, I set aside every March 2—the anniversary date of my abortion—for fasting and prayer, thanking God for His incredible mercy and beseeching Him that hearts might recognize abortion for what it is—the slaughtering of innocent babies. As of the date of this writing, approximately fifty million defenseless lives in the United States alone have been mercilessly cut short.

Jerry and I were raised in different religious denominations, resulting in differing beliefs between us. Consequently, for the first five years of our marriage we did not attend church. It seemed easier to avoid this area rather than risk the controversy and strife. However, strife ensued anyway, as it was impossible to avoid discussions of God or religion altogether.

When our children were one and two years old, I began to experience a lot of unrest. We needed to start going to church. But would Jerry be open? If so, which church should we attend?

Through family and friends, I heard of the Church On the Way, with Pastor Jack Hayford. I heard good things—people were being challenged to grow in their walk with Christ. To my surprise, Jerry agreed to give the Church On the Way a try. We knew on our first visit that this was what we needed.

I gleaned much from Pastor Hayford's teaching and grew in the Lord at a rate I had not previously known. The contemporary and open worship style was unlike anything I was accustomed to. I found it to be much-needed life for my spiritually dry heart and soul. Once again, God began to remind me of His intent to use me in a particular work. There was no doubt in my mind that He would one day be working through me. At the time, I still believed I would be a missionary in some far-off land in the far future.

I was also convinced that nurturing my children and encouraging in them a love for Jesus was my primary ministry during this season of my life. I believed with all earnestness that any other mission field in my lifetime would forever pale in comparison. Yet in spite of this strong awareness, I fell short. In many ways I believe I was a good mom, but I did not face up to the difficulties I was experiencing with my husband as I should have. My heart had grown so bitter. I did not honor my children's father as I should have.

Still, my God has been faithful. How I thank Him for the remarkable adults my children are today! His Word tells us that He looks upon the heart. I believe He has seen my heart over the years and has honored my prayers and efforts—as meager as they have been—and has graciously filled in the gaps.

Chapter Seven

WE NOW ATTENDED church regularly and were receiving great teaching. Although my joy in Jesus was being renewed, I battled with depression and disappointment. My marriage was still not what it should be. My husband's relationship with his children was not what it should be.

The rubble from the abortion loomed over my life. It constantly simmered on a back burner of my mind and almost continuously pricked my heart. I became a master at masking the pain and sadness which dwelt inside me. I fought hard to conceal the gloomy cloud that was as much a part of me as the beating of my heart.

I once read a quote that impressed itself upon my heart. It implied that the joy of a mother is crucial to the healthy development of her child. While knowing that Jesus is the key to ultimate and lasting joy, I was also aware that the impact I had on my children's lives was also of great significance. Being a joyful mother was not hard—I truly found it joyful. Yet I'm sure some of my sadness must have been projected, as well.

Thankfully, my God is bigger. In Him, I have always found joy, even if at times that joy has been clouded. I have always had hope, even if at times I have felt only a flicker. I have always found the strength I need, and even if at times that strength was scarce, it has always been enough.

When my daughter was very young, I began having disturbing dreams of her nearly drowning, to be rescued just in the nick of time. On numerous nights, this dream replayed itself. These dreams continued for a couple of years.

One Sunday afternoon, my mom telephoned. She told me of a troublesome dream she had dreamed the night before. Immediately following our conversation, the telephone rang again. It was my sister. She related to me an alarming dream she had had the night before also. I was speechless and frightened. Their dreams were identical to the dreams that were troubling me, and which I too had experienced the night before.

I sought a pastor at our church for insight. He believed the dreams might be a warning from God, and suggested extra prayer coverage for my daughter. He then offered to pray with me. Afterward, he shared that while praying, he saw a picture of Jesus standing alongside my daughter, wearing a coat of all the colors of the rainbow. He understood this to be an assurance of God's protection.

Within a couple of weeks of talking and praying with the pastor, my world came crashing down. My brother Doug was attending a Bible College fairly close to Jerry's and my home. He often spent the weekends with us, sometimes bringing a friend or two along. On one such visit, Doug brought along two friends I had not met before. I was in the kitchen cleaning up after dinner when one of these friends approached me.

"Did you hear what your daughter just told me?"

I turned and listened numbly as the details came out. I felt the color rush from my face and turned back to the sink. Nausea overtook me. My sweet, three-year-old daughter had been sexually violated—on numerous occasions—by my fifteen-year-old cousin. He was the son of the uncle who had sexually violated me!

I took Jerry aside into our bedroom and told him everything. Later that evening, when I was giving our daughter a bath, I asked her as naturally as possible about the times when she and my cousin played. She timidly told me the same things I had already heard. Then she added that my cousin had threatened to physically harm her if she ever told me the things he had done to her. He warned her that if I ever found out, I would be so mad at her that I would leave her. I then understood why my daughter had told a stranger rather than me of her sexual abuse. She was afraid I would be mad at her and leave her.

Initially I felt mainly sad, confused, and repulsed. There were certain details that now began to make sense. For no apparent reason, my daughter had begun wetting her bed at night, after not having done so for months. She was having difficulties making it to her toilet chair in time during the day, as well. I had assumed this was just a phase, as she was still young. She had also become excessively clingy with me and whiny, which was completely out of character. I now recognized these behavioral changes as an emotional cry for help.

My heart ached as though a dagger had been thrust all the way through. It was not long before anger filled my being. How dare my cousin threaten my daughter or tell her I would leave her! I lashed out at God, asking why and how this could have happened.

My children and I had visited my aunt from time to time, but only when my uncle was at work. He was the one I was wary of. I had never left my children alone with my cousin. He was not always home when we visited, but when he was, he played with my children. They'd pop in and out of the room where my aunt and I were visiting. I'd hear their voices as they played. At the time, having no idea what was actually going on, I thought it was sweet of my cousin to take the time to play with my kids. Now, the thought disgusts me.

One of the most exasperating parts of this whole travesty was how little we could do in response. When caught up in the throngs of this horrendous ordeal, there wasn't really anything we could do to retaliate or to undo the damage which had been done.

The morning after we learned of our daughter's abuse, Jerry telephoned my aunt. He requested that she, my uncle, and my cousin all be home that evening, as he needed to speak with them.

That evening, Jerry voiced his plan of revenge as he stormed out our front door.

I pleaded with him not to do anything rash. I did not want my husband, our children's father, to end up in jail. Our daughter's life had already been traumatized enough.

I have never felt so helpless and alone as when I sat on the sofa after Jerry walked out that door. I slapped the palms of my hands against the coffee table until they stung, crying out to God, "*Why?*"

I had prayed many times that my daughter would never be violated in the way I had been. Bitterly I asked myself, *Why had I even bothered? What had been the point to all my prayers? How could God allow this to happen when I had so earnestly prayed that it wouldn't?*

Angry and hurt, I withdrew from God. I stopped reading my Bible and quit praying. The One I most needed to turn to, I turned away from. I felt forsaken and betrayed.

By the time Jerry arrived at my aunt and uncle's home that evening, they and my cousin were all in tears. My cousin had told his parents everything, even expanding on what we already knew. Thankfully, Jerry refrained from harming my cousin. That would have only made an already terrible situation even worse.

Jerry and I filed a police report and had my cousin arrested. He was taken to the police station and questioned. With some hesitancy, we chose not to press charges. The way the laws stood in California at the time, our daughter would have had to testify. My aunt and uncle would probably have hired the best attorney, as they were financially able to do so. Jerry and I imagined our three-year-old daughter sitting up on the witness seat, distressed and in tears. We were not willing to put her through that.

Upon our insistence, however, my cousin did go through one year of counseling. An associate pastor from our church spoke with our daughter on one occasion, with me present. He then referred her to a counseling center that dealt solely with abused children.

One night, a month or two after the discovery of my daughter's abuse, I experienced a dream in which I was being sucked farther and farther into a long, dark tunnel. In the dream, a train whistle bellowed louder and louder. I felt overpowered and out of control. At the end of the tunnel I saw light, and as I approached it, I encountered peace. "Thy word is a lamp unto my feet and a light unto my path," spoke a male voice, calm and steady.

I awoke with a strong prompting to open my bedside table drawer and pull out my Bible, which I had stuffed inside weeks before. I opened it and Psalm 119:105 jumped out at me. "Thy word is a lamp unto my feet and a light unto my path" (KJV).

I knew God had led me to this passage because I had no clue where it was located. Feeling compelled, I got up and turned on the radio in the living room. I slumped to the carpet in tears as Amy Grant's voice richly sang, "Thy word is a lamp unto my feet and a light unto my path ..."

"Oh, my sweet Jesus, help me. I've missed you so," I cried, kneeling with my face toward the carpet and rocking back and forth. In my despair, I had fled from my Stronghold, my one true Anchor. I had resolved to get through on my own. This proved to be foolhardy. I discovered that apart from Him, I was hopeless, and there was no healing and no peace.

Through that verse in Psalms, God shed His light onto the sorrow and the gloominess of my soul. He assured me that although I had felt alone and forsaken, I had never been abandoned. He was redirecting me to His Word, my only hope.

A short time later, Doug telephoned from Bible college. He said he believed God had given him a word intended for me: "God will someday use you in a ministry for grieving women, if you will be open to it."

Okay, I hesitantly thought to myself, *Sounds good, but how and when?*

I was a quiet housewife, shrouded with a lack of self-confidence. I still had a long way to go in my walk with the Lord. Although I could not begin to fathom how this ministry would be realized, I felt confident in my spirit that this was indeed from God. I think it is noteworthy to add here that this type of communication between my brother and me is not a common occurrence. Neither before nor since has he expressed any such revelation to me.

On a Sunday evening not long afterward, the "Lambs" children's choir sang for the congregation. Following their performance, I hugged my children and told them how wonderfully they had sung.

"Mommy, Mommy, did you see Jesus?" beamed my daughter. "He was standing right next to me while I was singing. He was wearing a beautiful rainbow coat."

No, I had not seen Him … with my eyes. But my spirit recognized that my daughter seeing Him was a clear confirmation of the picture the pastor had received during the time we had prayed together. I felt like I had just received a huge hug from my Lord. The dreams of my daughter's impending drowning had been a warning of her sexual abuse. But God had rescued her! He had been there all along and would continue to keep her.

One afternoon during that same time period, I was in our backyard, shutting off the valve to the garden hose. The sound of birds' wings fluttered overhead. I raised my eyes, but saw no bird. Instead, a radiant circle of light shone through the tree branches. Immediately, the thought of a dove symbolizing the Holy Spirit came to mind. Along with that came the comfort and assurance that He had been with me at every point and would continue to be in the midst of whatever I was going through. If we have given our heart to Jesus, we are never alone. He is always there to see us through.

With everything coming to light in regards to my daughter's sexual abuse, other things came out in the open as well. My aunt had not known of my uncle's sexual abuse toward me until one afternoon during an emotional conversation over the phone.

I had not intended to divulge what had been so carefully guarded for so many years. I loved my aunt and had no desire to cause her pain. However, after listening with frustration as she rationalized her son's behavior one more time, I could not restrain myself. It all came billowing out. I shook with alarm as I realized what my lips had spewed forth. My aunt was shocked and angry that she had not known any of this.

My parents had chosen not to tell my aunt those many years ago, desiring to spare her hurt. My uncle had sworn to my dad that nothing of this nature would occur again, and my dad had taken him at his word. My parents did not learn until years later that my uncle had broken his word. After that first incidence of sexual abuse, the humiliation and awkwardness I felt with subsequent occurrences caused me to keep it all inside. I felt so dirty and ashamed.

My parents handled the situation in the best way they knew how. My uncle's first betrayal was back in the mid-1960s. This subject was not out in the open like it is today. Nobody talked about sexual abuse toward children in those days.

The pastor with whom my dad sought counsel told him that no one had ever approached him with this type of situation before. He admitted that he did not feel qualified to deal with such a delicate situation.

One evening my aunt, my uncle, Jerry, and I met for counsel and mediation with a pastor at the Church On the Way. It was a heart-wrenching and tearful session. My uncle cried, begging for my forgiveness. When it was over, my aunt stormed out of the room—angry, confused, and hurt. I watched as she hurried out into the dark winter night. She looked so terribly alone. I ached for the injustice that had befallen her.

I have been asked how I could forgive my uncle and my cousin for their disgrace toward my daughter and me. I cannot say that in and of myself I have the ability to forgive others who have brought me or those I love harm. It is only the grace of Jesus Christ working in me that makes this possible. I cannot say that I have not wrestled with and harbored anger toward those who have hurt me. I have! I do not always want to release my feelings of ill will. In some twisted way it feels satisfying sometimes to be angry at someone. But I have discovered that this sense of satisfaction is fleeting.

It is at such times that God lovingly reminds me of the many times I have hurt Him; of the countless times He has responded to *my* cries for mercy. I can't count the number of times He has picked me up, brushed me off, and given me a fresh start. He has forgiven me for so much. How can I not forgive others? This is the ideal, but it is a battle I win only when I submit myself fully to His Lordship.

There was a time when I assumed I deserved to be rewarded with a smooth and pleasant existence just for being a Christian, especially if I was a *good* Christian. Eventually I came to a point, however, where I realized that for the vast majority of the time I was not even that—a good Christian.

I have also come to realize Jesus never promised His followers a life of ease. In fact, His Word tells us to expect just the opposite. John 16:33 tells us that in this world we will have troubles. God does not promise to shield us from all difficulty, but He does promise to walk right beside us.

I love this passage from the book of Isaiah: "I will not forget you! See, I have engraved you on the palms of my hands" (Isaiah 49:14-16). His nail scars testify of His endless love.

First Peter 1:6-7 exhorts: "In this you greatly rejoice, though now for a little while you may have had to suffer grief in all kinds of trials. These have come so that your faith-of greater worth than gold, which perishes even though refined by fire, may be proved genuine and may result in praise, glory and honor when Jesus Christ is revealed."

Hard times require much faith on my part to accept that God is in control and that He really does have my best interests at heart. I am often well down the road before I am able to look back and recognize His hand at work.

The book of Psalms reads: "For you, O God tested us; you refined us like silver. You brought us into prison and laid burdens on our backs. You let men ride over our heads; we went through fire and water, but you brought us to a place of abundance" (Psalm 66:10-12).

The best response for me in these times is to first acknowledge my feelings of anger, hurt, helplessness, or whatever it may be, and then turn to God with the mindset: *I can't do this on my own, Lord. This hurts way too much. This is too hard. Please take it and deal with it for me.* It is then I find the peace only He can give.

I would not choose to relive the difficult times I have experienced; nevertheless I am thankful that through them I have gained a deeper appreciation for God's amazing grace and for Jesus' precious blood.

I have grown far more through suffering than through ease. It is when I have been at my lowest point and have turned desperately to my God that I have experienced Him the most deeply. Jesus, the One who suffered beyond my comprehension, has consistently provided me comfort. Time and time again, He has come through for me in the desert, always taking me to the other side. What a wonderful Redeemer He is!

Chapter Eight

I HAD NOT EXPERIENCED a strong sense of separation from my parents after they moved to Oregon, and yet I could not shake loose the belief that Oregon was where we were supposed to be.

Now and then I brought up the idea to Jerry, but he was hesitant. He had steady work as an electrician in Southern California, and we were blessed with a comfortable and secure life. Jerry tends to be the practical one, while I am somewhat idealistic. I entertained this fanciful notion of a perfect storybook life in the great Northwest. Yet when we finally moved to Oregon, my notion was quickly dashed. I found people to be people, their morality as broken as with people everywhere.

Finalizing the decision to move to Oregon was significant. Our life in California was established. Our kids attended a private Christian school. Through their school, our church, and the neighborhood, they had developed close friendships. We had a nice home, with a large yard and swimming pool, in a nice neighborhood. Although our marriage and family life were not ideal, from a practical standpoint, life was good.

Yet the pull to Oregon was persistent.

While still living in California, God began rekindling in my heart the desire to become a nurse. I had toyed with the idea right out of high school, then quickly changed my plans after Jerry and I became engaged, enrolling in a medical assisting course instead. This course took seven months rather than the several years required to earn a registered nurse's license.

My dad had tried to persuade me—right up to the morning of our wedding—to put the marriage on hold and complete nursing school first. He even offered to pay the tuition.

"No, I just want to get married and have babies," I responded.

Many years later, God stirred a fresh call to nursing. I enrolled in prerequisite classes at a nearby community college. This time the financial responsibility was on us. Maybe I should have listened to my father, after all.

Two weeks into the school term, our house, which had been on the real estate market for over one year, sold. I withdrew from my classes. I had thought there would be time for me to complete that spring term. God had other ideas and, as usual, His timeline differed from mine.

One evening, out of the blue, Jerry came home from work and announced that it was time to move to Oregon. All of his previous doubts were apparently gone. I was taken aback by this change. But I was also pleased. It affirmed what I had been feeling for years.

So, thirteen years after my parents and siblings moved to Oregon, my husband and I packed up our children and followed. As we drove away that late March morning, we waved good-bye to the friends and neighbors who had come to wish us well. Max, our much-loved golden retriever, sat behind the back seat of our jeep.

It was incredibly bittersweet. We looked forward to what lay ahead, but it was also sad. The house we had lived in for over fourteen years backed up to the house I had grown up in. For our children, who were twelve and ten-and-a-half years old, this was the only home they had ever known.

It felt strange driving away from our home and realizing that we would not be returning. Others would now call this place home, and that did not sit right with me. Riding along that oh-so-familiar street, and passing the houses and yards that had become so ingrained in my mind, was unsettling. As we waited at the stop light to get onto the freeway, I did not experience that same sense of hurry I always had. Instead, I felt an almost panicky feeling to stop and reverse everything. I found myself wishing I would awaken and find it had all been a dream. But it was not a dream. It was the dawn of a whole new life, a life I am convinced was part of God's plan and leading.

Not long after our move to Oregon, I enrolled in classes at Portland Community College. I was still drawn to nursing. It had been a long time since I had attended school, and based on the enrollment placement tests, I was required to start at the beginning for practically everything.

It was often trying, sitting through many of the lectures, as the secular world's views were repeatedly hammered, whether the listeners agreed with the instructor or not. It seemed unfair that the instructor could hold this type of power. I was grounded enough spiritually not to be swayed, but what about those students who were not so grounded? I saw many followers on that campus; few seemed willing to stand apart.

During one medical ethics class session, the instructor asked if any students would refuse to work in an abortion clinic based on their religious or ethical beliefs, if it were the only job available; if it meant they or their children would go hungry if they did not take the job. Out of roughly fifty students, I was the only one who raised my hand. All eyes turned to me as the instructor zeroed in on his target.

"Give me wisdom, Jesus," I prayed softly.

God was kind to me that day. The conversation quickly became side-tracked and stayed on an entirely different topic until the bell rang.

One morning the topic in one of my biology classes was birth control. The instructor laid out every conceivable method which—according to her—was "acceptable and responsible."

The student sitting next to me raised her hand. "There is one method of birth control you have failed to mention—abstinence."

The instructor raised her eyebrows and chuckled, which was the extent of her response. Then she posed a question to the students. "If your unborn baby were diagnosed with a chronic condition that forced him or her to live a life of misery and pain, would you expose your baby to a wretched life? Or would you compassionately choose to terminate that pregnancy?"

The consensus of my fellow classmates was that it would be selfish and unloving on the mother's part *not* to have an abortion.

I could not keep from raising my hand. "Would any of you have your *newborn* killed if he or she were born with a debilitating condition?" I paused. "What's the difference?"

This began a heartfelt dialogue, where I was accused in the end of being insensitive and unloving, someone who would permit my child to live a life of misery rather than exercise my right to prevent his or her birth altogether. As

I sat there with my peers, I pondered at how twisted and far removed from God's truths the thinking of this world had become.

During that same hour, a student whom I had not previously heard speak out told of her younger sister who had been born with a brittle bone disease that could result in a break at any given time, with little provocation. She described how her sister, who was only twelve years old, had already experienced multiple fractured bones. Her eyes moistened as she told her story.

"I have never known a happier person in my life than my sister. She is the one who is continually encouraging everybody else. She is our angel. I know she is grateful our mother gave her life. We are all very grateful to have her in our family."

Her story didn't appear to sway the instructor's or any of the student's opinion.

"Well, most disabled children do not have such a positive outcome. And I still don't think it is fair to your sister to live a pain-filled life," responded the instructor.

I saw several students' heads nodding in agreement. Nobody spoke out to disagree.

The entire college scene was a remarkable adventure for me. I was certain I would be the oldest student on campus. I was pleasantly surprised and relieved to discover I was just one of *many* older students.

Tears streamed down my face one Sunday morning when a young mother shared with the congregation how she had been unwed and pregnant and resolved to abort her baby until a friend steered her to a place called the Pregnancy Resource Centers. Holding her baby in her arms, the young woman stood there, praising God for the caring support she had received through the Pregnancy Resource Centers. Their support had resulted in her choosing life for her baby.

This was the first I had heard of the Pregnancy Resource Centers. I was completely unaware that morning how greatly my life would be impacted as a result. The next morning, I telephoned the number listed in the church bulletin for the PRC closest to my home.

"I want to volunteer," I announced to the woman who answered the phone. She transferred me to the Center Director, who scheduled a time for me to come to the center and meet with her. The next week, during the course of our conversation, the director asked how I felt about abortion. As part of my response, I told her about my own abortion. She graciously informed me that I would need to complete PRCs' post-abortion support group before I would be eligible to volunteer.

This was not what I had expected—or wanted—to hear. I was not particularly keen on the idea. The last thing I wanted to do was sit around with a bunch of women I did not know and rehash my abortion.

With much reluctance, I looked further into this post-abortion support group, HEART (which stands for Healing Encouragement for Abortion-Related Trauma). It proved to be one of the best decisions of my life. Through HEART, I found full healing and restoration in Jesus Christ.

The healing process was arduous, yet very necessary in order to come to a place of rest, and to a place where at last I was able to forgive myself. More importantly, to a place where I was finally able to gratefully accept Christ's forgiveness. I walked away from HEART with the confidence that my baby is in heaven with Jesus, and that someday we will be reunited. How I look forward to that day!

After seventeen years of hurting and grieving, I was finally at peace with my abortion. The repeated emotional lashings I had been inflicting on myself, as well as the nightmares and depression, ended.

I would undo my abortion if I could. But today, the joy is much stronger than the pain. My recognition of my need for a Savior is so much greater. My appreciation for His love and forgiveness holds such greater significance.

My son Eric's name, along with words of personal sentiment, now adorns a plaque mounted on a wall at the National Memorial for the Unborn in Chattanooga, Tennessee, as well as at the Memorial for the Unborn in Newberg, Oregon. God has truly turned my mourning and ashes into joy and thanksgiving, and today He is using me in ways that would not be possible otherwise.

Chapter Nine

IN SPITE OF the healing I had experienced through HEART, life on the home front was still not good. After three years of prerequisites, I was accepted into nursing school, only to decline. After nineteen years of marriage, the children and I moved out of our home. I was at a place of utter weariness and could not go on any longer with the way things were. The day I left Jerry, my heart was set on divorce. I contacted an attorney. I was finished.

Almost immediately following our separation, my brother Doug telephoned to say he had scheduled an appointment for me to meet with a counselor at his church.

Doug carried on about how "God must have orchestrated all of this" because the church secretary was able to fit me in the very next day. He added, "This counselor typically has to be scheduled weeks in advance."

I was annoyed. How intrusive for Doug to arrange all of this behind my back! I was certain I would hear this woman tell me I needed to be a good Christian wife, pack my bags, and return home to my husband.

"My car is in for repairs for the next couple of days. I won't be able to go," I replied, relieved at having a way out.

Doug cheerfully retorted that his wife would pick me up. The next morning, I rode in their van en route to my appointment. Looking at the shriveled-up French fries all over the van floor, I felt like a child, silently grumbling, as if I was being forced into doing something I did not want to do.

Twenty minutes into my first session with Jean at Beaverton Foursquare Church, she leaned forward in her seat and looked intently into my eyes. "You should have left years ago."

Her response caught me completely off guard. Any discomfort I had felt toward Jean earlier instantly disappeared. I felt comfortable with her from then on. She held fast to her belief that I did not have biblical grounds for divorce, but she *did* believe a separation was in order.

Jean encouraged me to ask Jerry to join us for counseling. When I hesitantly asked him over the phone one evening, he agreed. I expected the primary focus of our sessions together to be how Jerry needed to change. Jean, however, pointed out ways in which I had been at fault as well, which I was not so pleased with at first. Yet once I took a deep breath and allowed my heart to hear what Jean was saying, I began to recognize how hard my heart had grown towards my husband; and how my anger towards him had aided in building the wall between us.

Spiritually, I grew tremendously during this time. I cried out to God for wisdom, and for His will—and not mine—to be realized. I began praying in a manner I had never done before. Rather than listing to God all the ways in which I felt my husband needed to change, I began asking God to help me see my husband the way *He* sees him, and to love my husband the way *He* loves him. Amazingly, my heart and attitude started to change. I began seeing Jerry through softer eyes, and with a gentler heart.

Although receiving Christian counseling during this time was beneficial, it was not as effective as pouring myself into God's Word and earnestly seeking His face. Among other insights, God began to show me that I had not been loving my husband as I should, that I was to love and honor my husband, *period*, without any buts or exceptions, regardless of my opinions, regardless of whether or not I considered him deserving of my honor. By harboring bitterness and not truly loving my husband, I was not being obedient to Christ.

At first this seemed unfair, as if I had been dealt the bum end of the deal.

"But what about *him*, Lord?" I sniveled.

As I genuinely sought God and made an effort to obey Him, however, the resentment and the pain began to lift. It was not easy, nor was it an instant cure-all. It was quite difficult and would prove to be a very long process.

At the start of our marriage, I had determined to please my husband. But before long, disappointment set in, and slowly my heart hardened. With time, anger and resentment festered. Rather than confronting these head-on, which would have been best, I rationalized and fed my resentment. I knew in my heart these attitudes were not right, but it was through them I found a twisted means of coping, a distorted sort of release. It was during our time of separation that their grip, which I had allowed to encrust my heart for so many years, began to loosen.

The change in me, however, took (regrettably) a long time. Years following our separation and reconciliation, God once again had to admonish me. I was still not loving my husband as I should. My grasp had become much looser, but I was still holding on to deeply embedded, destructive feelings.

And I had to forgive my husband for his part in the abortion. I had to forgive him for not stopping me from going through with the abortion—for not protecting our child—for not protecting me. I had to forgive him for writing the check to pay for the abortion. The importance of forgiveness is addressed in PRC's post-abortion support group—but for me, fully forgiving my husband took a long time. I've heard the post-abortion healing journey likened to the peeling of an onion ... the process taking place layer by layer.

God showed me how my own children had been marred by my bitter resolve. Above all, He showed me I had been sinning against *Him*. God used one of my dear children to help make it clear. During a time of great pain, I threw myself at the feet of Jesus in prayer, reflection, and repentance. In return, I received an abundant outpouring of God's love and grace. As difficult as it was, I would not trade one tear or heartfelt sting for the good it brought. It took this tough time to bring me to the place I am today, where I can honestly say my heart is right in regards to my husband.

I am thankful today that our separation did not end in divorce. Our marriage is better now than I ever believed possible. The union I once resented is a joy; my love for my husband is true and deep.

I am determined not to go back to where I was for far too long. Rather than allowing myself to dwell on the hardships that *still* arise, I focus on Christ and on how I am to honor Him in all things, which includes unselfishly loving my husband.

To be fair to my husband, he is not the same man today as the one I once walked out on. God has significantly transformed his heart as well.

Shortly after Jerry and I reunited, I reapplied to nursing school. Two and a half years later, at the age of forty years and eleven months, I graduated as a registered nurse.

I had the largest support group in the audience. "Looks like you brought the whole town with you," one of the instructors teased as she handed me my diploma. I proudly waved at my loudly cheering family members, piled into two long rows of chairs. I could hear my dad's voice and whistle above all the others.

In spite of numerous times of frustration during nursing school, I am thankful I didn't give up. I never seriously considered giving up, always certain I would (eventually) arrive at my goal. I believe this confidence and motivation came from God, as it was all part of His larger plan for my life.

In order to become licensed as a Registered Nurse, I had to pass the state exam. That exam was stressful, to say the least. I had studied, studied, and studied some more. When it came to the actual test day and I realized I was taking the real thing, my mind pretty much went blank.

The next several weeks felt like months while I waited for the results. When they finally came in the mail, I hurried up the driveway, waving my long-sought-after prize at Jerry. In spite of my fear that I had failed the test, I passed with flying colors.

Not long afterwards, I acquired a full-time nursing position. It was an adjustment. I had been a housewife for eighteen years before entering nursing school. My new job proved to be physically, mentally, and emotionally demanding, but also extremely satisfying. As draining as it has been at times, I have never doubted for a moment that nursing is where I am meant to be.

Chapter Ten

ONE SUNDAY MORNING, Jerry and I were visiting a church for the first time; it was communion Sunday. The pastor invited the congregation to come to the front of the church a couple of rows at a time to receive communion. As we did, the pastor and a woman named Mary briefly prayed for or spoke to each of us.

Mary placed her hand on my forehead and quietly said, "Your feet are planted firmly on the Rock."

I felt a rush. I had never received an affirmation quite like this before. I also pondered to myself, *Who, me?* My feet were anything *but* firm. I was taken aback to hear that God perceived me this way.

When we sat down, Jerry told me Mary had asked him if we would stay after the service. She wanted to talk with me. Following the service, with Jerry at my side, I approached Mary. I had never met her before this day. We sat down, and Mary told me that as she approached me during communion she had sensed God speaking these words: "*Rock woman. Rock woman.*"

"Your feet are planted firmly on the Rock, Jesus Christ," she said confidently. Then Mary shared that she believed God was speaking to her the following words, intended for me: "God will be using you in a ministry for grieving women, and events will progress very rapidly."

I lost it. Mumbling through uncontrollable tears, I told her about my abortion, as well as my own and my daughter's past sexual abuse. I also told her how I had received an identical word through my brother sixteen years earlier.

It could not be coincidence that I had received the same word from God, from two people who had no knowledge of each other, in two completely different places in my life, in two different states, sixteen years apart. I left that place with an overwhelming sense of excitement and expectation.

"Whatever you have in store for me, wherever you want me to go, whatever you want me to do, I am open, Lord," I prayed.

Shortly afterwards, while driving along the highway, I was listening to a song entitled "So Great Is Your Mercy." As rain spattered against the windshield, I was overcome with the awareness of how very merciful and gracious God had been toward me. With each word that He had given me of His plan to use me in a ministry for grieving women, He had laid out a timeline. The first time, He had said His plan would come together "someday." The second time, He had emphasized, "Events will progress very rapidly."

When I had first received this word from God, He had added that He would use me, if I were open to it. At the time, I needed a lot of clean-up in my heart and emotions, and particularly in my walk with Jesus. It was necessary that I come to a place of total, unwavering surrender; to be set free from past bondage. The second time I was at a much better place emotionally, spiritually, and practically.

God also made it plain that when He had spoken to me through a dream, through His Word, and through a song on the radio, that His "Word is a lamp unto my feet and a light unto my path," that He was not only healing and setting me free from the shackles and the pain of my daughter's and my own past sexual abuse, but He was also equipping me for the work He was calling me to.

All along, He had a plan. He had pulled me out of a dark and slippery pit, grounded my feet on the Rock, and put true joy back in my heart. I sensed God impressing on me that His love is so great and His purpose so important that He was not about to allow His plans to be thwarted or His timeline to be altered.

After receiving that affirmation from God through Mary, I continued working as a hospital nurse, while waiting in wonder to see God's plan fulfilled.

My sister, Kathy, has volunteered a number of years at the Royal Family Kid's Camp, a summer camp for abused children placed in foster care. Listening to my sister tell of her experiences, I felt drawn to volunteer.

Kathy, as co-counselor, and I shared a cabin with four girls for a stirring and amazing week.

One afternoon, the campers were asked to write down their goals for adulthood. One of our girls wrote, "I hope I will not hurt my own children someday."

Another wrote, "I hope I will be a responsible parent and that my kids will be proud of me."

This same afternoon during a break, Kathy, our girls, and I sat on a blanket under a tree. One of the girls again expressed her fear that she would be incapable of being a good parent, that she may one day abuse her own children. Sadly she had been abused both physically and sexually numerous times in her young life.

I shared my own story of sexual abuse and told her she did not have to go down the same path she had known. Through Jesus, the cycle could be broken. Each child left RFKC having heard daily that Jesus loves them and how through Him they can overcome.

Two years later, this young girl was brutally murdered by one more man who had presented himself as trustworthy. She is now safe with her heavenly Father, who will never betray her. Never again will she be let down by this dark and sinful world.

Although I had been blessed by and enjoyed being a part of Royal Family Kid's Camp, I awoke one night with the overwhelming feeling that God did not want me to return as a counselor the next year.

I had no peace about this until I called the camp director the following morning and told him I would not be available to volunteer the next year.

It had been almost one year since that Sunday when God had spoken to me through Mary. I was beginning to grow discouraged. Nothing seemed to be progressing "very rapidly" as Mary had said.

"Lord, events don't seem to be progressing 'very rapidly' here," I prayed.

About five months later my friend Lou, whom I had met in nursing school, telephoned me. "The Pregnancy Resource Centers are going to be hiring a third ultrasound nurse. Let's apply."

My heart leaped with hope. Until now, I had not been aware of PRC's ultrasound ministry. I had not had further involvement with PRC since graduating from HEART eight years before. At that time, the ultrasound ministry had not yet been established.

Lou and I met for lunch later that week and then went into the nearest PRC. Sue, the center's director, gave Lou and me a tour of the center. She informed us our first step was to apply to volunteer as a counselor. If accepted, we would need to complete the upcoming training course. She gave us applications to take home. I filled mine out that evening.

Once she had received my application and letters of reference, Sue scheduled an interview with her and a time when I could meet with Diana, PRC's then nurse manager. Following my interview with Sue, I was offered a position as a volunteer counselor. Sue introduced me to Diana, who kindly explained that the next nurse would be hired from the volunteer counselor pool. Due to budget constraints, however, the hiring had been put on hold for an unknown period of time.

I felt discouraged. Why was there always some kind of glitch? I proceeded with the volunteer counselor training. My friend Lou decided she was not convinced of God's call to the ministry of PRC.

Looking back, I can see how God patiently brought His plans to pass. According to my idea of time, God was moving slowly. According to His perfect timing, however, events came together at exactly the right time.

Approximately eight years after God first told me His intent to use me in a ministry for grieving women, He led me to HEART. This was imperative before I would be ready for the next step.

He then coaxed me toward—and got me through— nursing school. I give Him all the credit, because in my own strength and ability, I don't think I would have made it.

It was eight years following HEART, and three years after completing nursing school, before I had further involvement with PRC. After completing PRC's volunteer counselor training, I again had to wait on the Lord. But this wait was much shorter. After about four months of volunteering as a counselor one morning a week, Diana approached me. "There is a nursing position opening up. Would you like to apply?"

"Yes!"

Diana scheduled an interview with the then Director of Centers, Annie, and herself. Diana told me they would not make their decision right away, as there were other applicants to be considered and another interview after me. I had no option but to leave it in the Lord's hands. Toward the close of my interview with Annie and Diana, they told me they had made their decision. I was offered the position! I felt excited and in awe at how God was orchestrating everything. The three of us then prayed together.

One month later, I was flown to Torrance, California, for ultrasound instruction through CareNet, the national umbrella organization that covers the Pregnancy Resource Centers. That week was a thrilling one. I had the opportunity to meet many others with a passion for the unborn. I even met Amy Grant's father. Dr. Grant was—at the time—the medical director for a CareNet center in Tennessee. I had the privilege of sitting and talking with him during one of our lunch breaks. It was an honor. I did not tell Dr. Grant how profoundly God had ministered to me through his daughter singing "Thy Word," but meeting Amy's earthly father did much to encourage me.

My ultrasound training took place during the same week as Royal Family Kid's Camp that year. It would have been impossible to have done both. I now understood the reason for the strong impression that I was not to volunteer as a counselor that year for RFKC.

I did volunteer, however, the following year as a relief nurse for RFKC in the evenings, after working during the day for PRC. God is so faithful to work out the details. I have come to discover that all He asks of us is a willing and obedient heart.

Chapter Eleven

FOLLOWING MY ULTRASOUND training in California, I trained beside Diana for the next four months. Although I grew to love and admire Diana, and enjoyed working closely with her, I grew anxious to be on my own. By the time my training was over, I felt more than ready.

I took a significant pay cut when I joined the staff of PRC, but am blessed with a husband who was and still is totally okay with that. However, both children were in college and we were paying their tuition. Jerry and I agreed that I would continue to work every other weekend at my nursing home job, as well as the four days a week for PRC.

I adhered to this schedule for a year and a half, during which time I experienced frequent head colds and constant fatigue. Diana periodically asked if I felt that both jobs were too much. I knew she was hinting that I should resign from my weekend job; but I was hesitant to let go. I loved hands-on nursing, and I was fearful of losing many of my nursing skills as well as the added income.

One morning during a PRC nurses' meeting, I was strongly encouraged by my peers to quit my weekend job. I sat there with a tissue in hand, attempting to blow my stuffed-up nose. I felt divided inside and resistant to their suggestion. My daughter was now engaged to be married. In seven months, she would be finished with school and married. Jerry and I felt I needed to continue my weekend job until then.

Toward the end of our meeting, we prayed together, asking for God's will to be made evident. Later, on my own, I repented to the Lord. I confessed that I had only half-heartedly sought His will, as I really did not want to quit my other job. Four months earlier I had resigned from the nursing home and returned to the hospital I had previously been employed with. The hospital was in need of a nurse to work every other weekend. I had made this change because the hospital position was easier physically than the nursing home position.

I asked God to close the door on the hospital job if He no longer desired me to work there.

Five days later, I received a telephone call from the staffing coordinator at the hospital, informing me the unit I had been working in would be permanently closing at the end of the month. Subsequently, my present position would no longer exist. Unless I was willing to work additional hours and various shifts, I was no longer needed.

Following that phone conversation, I sat for a few moments, stunned. I had sensed God speaking to me repeatedly that day while at PRC: "*I have led you here, now trust Me. I have led you here, now trust Me.*"

I *knew* He had led me to PRC. This telephone call confirmed it. Not only had God closed the door on my weekend job, He had *slammed* it shut.

I had been arranging my life, thinking I knew best, without sincerely taking time to seek God's will. And here He was, showing me that my plans were not at all the same as His. He was asking me to trust Him entirely. I chose to make PRC my only employment, and God worked out the rest. We were able to pay for everything without going into debt.

No monetary value can be placed on how blessed I have been by being exactly where I am. The following is one of many such examples:

One dreary, rainy Wednesday morning, a young woman came into one of the Pregnancy Resource Centers, seeking information regarding abortion as well as spiritual encouragement. I noticed her sitting on the sofa in the waiting area, looking weary. I remember feeling a bit weary myself that morning. I sensed the taunting snarl of the enemy once again badgering that I was too small to make any real difference in this ongoing battle for life.

Once in the counseling room, Leah, the weary looking young woman, told Tamara that she had come directly to PRC from an abortion clinic, where she had an appointment scheduled for an abortion. Leah went on to say that as she sat in the crowded waiting room of that abortion clinic, she suddenly felt sickened, realizing each woman sitting beside her was going to be having an abortion. Her heart panicked when the clinic's receptionist called her to the front desk and asked; "How do you plan to pay for this?"

"I'm not. I'm leaving," Leah answered, and she hastened out the door.

Tamara offered Leah an ultrasound. She also shared the gospel with her. As I sat and talked with Leah in the ultrasound room, I was overcome with an urgency to continue what had been laid out. I shared my testimony with Leah and told her of God's great love for her. I asked

Leah if she would like to have a personal relationship with Jesus Christ.

"Yes, I think that is what I need. There is a deep emptiness inside of me, which nothing seems to be able to fill."

Leah prayed out loud, professing Jesus as her personal Lord and Savior. Later, when I introduced her to her active baby on the ultrasound screen, she began to cry. "Is that my baby's heart beating?"

"Yes," I answered.

Leah looked up at the wall clock and said, "If I had not left that place this morning, my baby would not be alive right now. At four-thirty this morning I telephoned my mom and said, 'Mom, I am pregnant, and I'm going to have an abortion later this morning.'"

"'Well, I am just going to be praying all morning that you don't. You need to find yourself a good church,' my mom told me."

Leah left PRC that morning with pictures of her baby, a Bible, church referrals, and most importantly, a new relationship with Jesus Christ. She hugged both Tamara and me as she left the center. "Thank you for everything. I am so glad I came here today."

God obviously loves Leah and her baby very much. What an honor that God chose me as one of the stepping stones in leading her to Him! Another wonderful piece of this story is that the abortion clinic where Leah had been sits just around the corner from PRC's inner-city center in Portland. Leah could have gone there, but God led her to another PRC center, much farther away. God knew that there would not be a nurse available to do the ultrasound at the center in Portland that day.

I imagine Leah's mama on her knees all morning that Wednesday, passionately pleading for the life of her grandbaby. And I imagine all the angels in heaven joyously celebrating the gift of life.

God hears and answers the prayers of a mother's and a grandmother's heart. He not only saved the life of that baby, but He also saved the soul of the baby's mother. God is so much mightier than this battle that rages. One by one, lives are being saved. He is making a victorious and eternal difference, one life at a time.

As mothers, we must never cease to pray. God does look tenderly upon a mother's heart. I can personally attest to that.

Chapter Twelve

WHAT A BLESSED opportunity it is to share the love and hope that only Jesus can give with hurting and grieving women! What a privilege it is to introduce abortion-minded women to their babies on the ultrasound screen. Over ninety percent of the women receiving ultrasounds at PRC choose life for their babies.

I regularly observe God miraculously changing hearts of stone to hearts of flesh. I share my own testimony with these women, telling them how Jesus brought relief to my once-shattered heart. I tell them that no matter what has come before…there is hope, there is peace, and there is joy to be found in Jesus Christ.

I have discovered it is not necessary to cross the seas to minister to others in Jesus' name. This world is filled with lost and hurting people. Every neighborhood, workplace, schoolyard, city, and village on this planet is a mission field.

I am so thankful that God has been faithful in bringing His plan for my life to fulfillment, in spite of me. Satan has tried in many ways to block God's plan. But my God is so much mightier.

It is a thrill to know that God had a plan and a purpose for my life long before I was conceived in my mother's womb. He knew I would entangle my life in sin. He knew I would have an abortion. He planned to use me in the ministry of PRC right from the very beginning.

A friend once told me, "Maybe that is why God had you have an abortion, so He could use you in the way He is today."

At first, this statement shocked and angered me. My immediate instinct was to defend God. But I felt a clear check in my spirit and realized I could not begin to explain how God's sovereignty works into the decisions each of us makes. What I do understand, however, is that—based on God's Word—my choice to engage in pre-marital sex and then to compound that sin by having an abortion was in direct opposition to Him.

Many insist a woman should have the right to choose, that it is *her* body. But what about the body of the baby inside her? Why is it a criminal act to take the life of a baby seconds after it is born, but legal *before* it is born? Or even legal *as* the baby is being born? If that same mother arranged for the taking of her baby's life after its birth, she would be arrested and charged as a cold and heartless killer. Where is the logic or consistency?

A young woman twenty-four weeks pregnant sat before me in the counseling room, expressing her intent to have an abortion. It would be her fourth. I told her about the possible physical and emotional risks with repeated abortions. She shrugged her shoulders. "I want to have an abortion before I get too far into my pregnancy."

I explained how her baby was already well-developed and could survive with medical assistance if born that day.

Her demeanor was one of nonchalant indifference. She asked if I knew how the abortion procedure would be performed at this stage of pregnancy. I read to her word-for-word from one of PRC's brochures: the steps involved in a partial-birth abortion, the category her pregnancy fell into.

When I began to read, she asked, half smiling, "Is this the one where they put the seaweed in you to cause the pregnancy to terminate?"

I read her the rest of the story. As I read, her shoulders, which had been confidently erected, slouched. Her gaze shifted away from me. Her entire body shuddered, and her eyes filled with tears. "All they told me about was the seaweed and that I would fall asleep. They never told me the other part." She then disclosed that she had had a partial-birth abortion one year earlier.

Shouldn't a woman's right to choose include the right to know the whole truth?

Supreme Court judges—educated by the wisdom of man—ruled that abortion is a woman's right. There are those who believe that since abortion has been pronounced legal by the highest court in the land, then it must be all right.

But in Proverbs 14:12, God exhorts, "There is a way that seems right to a man, but in the end it leads to death." In Isaiah 10:1, He warns, "Woe unto them that decree unrighteous decrees" (KJV).

Did anyone pursuing a woman's rights ever stop to seek God and ask what *His* opinion is in regards to abortion? I listened as a woman, who just learned she was pregnant, freely aired her opinions regarding abortion and how she intended to exercise her "right" to terminate her pregnancy.

It was the end of the day, and my head felt foggy. I was tired—tired of hearing one more selfish opinion. I gently gave her this response. I know it was from the Lord because my brain was too fuzzy to think of it on my own:

"You have your opinion. I have my opinion. Everybody has an opinion. What do you think God's opinion is regarding abortion?"

This woman, who seemed to have plenty to say beforehand, suddenly sat there completely silent. Tears soon streamed from her eyes, soaking her face.

"Would you like me to read from the Bible what God's opinion is regarding abortion?"

She nodded.

I left the center late that day, after sharing God's opinion, directly from His Word, regarding the life of her unborn baby.

"Can I have one of those?" she asked as I shut the Bible I had taken from the shelf in the ultrasound room. She left that evening with pictures of her baby, a Bible in hand, and a new relationship with Jesus Christ.

I am overwhelmed when I think about how far God has brought me. My own abortion was supposed to be a secret.

Now nobody will ever have to know. It's all behind me, I sighed with relief those many years ago.

Now, almost every day, I tell women about my experience and regrets in regards to my abortion. I sit here today, writing my story for anyone who desires to read it. At the time of my abortion, this would have been unimaginable. God's ways are certainly not ours.

In Genesis 50:20, God tells us that what man has meant for evil, He can use for good—for the saving of many lives. I am grateful beyond description that the evil which was done in aborting my baby, God has transformed into good. As a result, many babies' lives are being saved, and many women are being spared the heartache I have known.

I believe abortion hurts women. I speak from personal experience. I am a woman who has been hurt by abortion. I work with other women, and I have counseled numerous women who have been hurt by abortion. I have friends who have been hurt by abortion. I once watched a televised political convention where women wore T-shirts that read, "I had an abortion."

It totally floored me. Were they proud of this?

Their purpose in parading this skeleton from their past was to make a point that they had personally chosen abortion and were now "okay." In other words, all that matters is how *they* are doing. It's all about the woman. The baby or anyone else who may have been affected by that decision are irrelevant. The sad repercussion is that other women will be deceived into believing abortion is "no big deal" and that if they make this choice for an unwanted pregnancy, they too will be "okay."

The question I cannot help but ask is, "Are these women *really* 'okay'?"

The only reason I am "okay" is because of Jesus. Apart from Him, I don't know how anyone could ever fully recover from an abortion.

There are many men who have been hurt by abortion, as well. What about their rights? Legally, they have little—if any—say in the matter. Their right to know and father their child is stripped from them. The Pregnancy Resource Centers offer a post-abortion support group for men.

And where do the grandparents and the brothers and sisters' rights fit in to all of this? Who considers *their* feelings or their grief? I have counseled clients with older children, who knew of their mother's pregnancy, which was later aborted. I wonder what explanation was given. Oh, how complicated we make our lives, and how others are hurt in the process, when we disregard God and His ways!

A hard truth God showed me many years after going through HEART is that I deprived my son and daughter of their brother. My son, from as far back as I can remember, wanted a brother. Is saying "I'm sorry" enough? I do not think so. What words could ever be enough?

Nevertheless, and as feeble as it may sound, I am sorry, so very, very sorry.

Chapter Thirteen

I CANNOT SPEAK FOR all women, but I can speak for myself and for many others I have spoken with and say that post-abortion stress is a very real issue.

There was one client whose emotional pain I can hardly imagine. She detailed to me—quite vividly—her experience with taking the abortion pill, RU486. In her own words: "I actually felt my baby leaving my body, and then I saw it with my own eyes, lying in the toilet. It was right there in front of me—my tiny, helpless, dead baby. That picture will forever be in my mind. I have not had a good night's sleep since. I don't know if I will ever recover. I killed my own baby. How can I recover?"

Another client, Liz, confidently explained, "The timing was all wrong. I made the best choice for all involved by terminating my last pregnancy."

During her ultrasound she remained completely silent for several minutes and then abruptly spoke: "Okay, I've seen all I need to see."

I stopped the ultrasound. The tears soon began to flow. Not only hers, but her boyfriend Adam's as well. "Look what we did! Look what we did!" Liz screamed at Adam.

Adam began to tremble and slumped into a chair.

Liz hopped down from the ultrasound table and lunged at him. She began beating her fists into his chest. "We killed our baby! We killed our baby!" She then crouched down onto the carpet and began to wail loudly. Adam joined her.

"Oh, dear God," I silently prayed, "help these two." I didn't know what to say or do next. "Lord, help me." I sensed God telling me to keep silent, that I was to allow Liz and Adam this time.

"I had no idea. Why didn't they tell us?" Adam cried out loud.

I still didn't know what to say. "*Just let them be*," the Lord prodded.

After what seemed a fairly long time, Liz suddenly turned to me. "How can you do this? How can you possibly do this work after having had an abortion yourself?"

"It is only because of Jesus," I answered quietly. By now, I was crying right along with them.

We eventually were able to talk. I told them more about Jesus and referred them to HEART. I have had no contact with Liz or Adam since, but am grateful they had begun to take responsibility for the outcome of their previous pregnancy, and that they had begun to voice their grief.

My friend Darlene and her husband were in our home for dinner one evening, when Darlene noticed a picture of an angel holding a sleeping baby, which hangs on the wall above my bedside table. Darlene went closer to get a better look, and her eyes rested on the tiny plaque at the bottom of the picture. This plaque is a duplicate of the one honoring my son Eric at the Memorial for the Unborn in

Oregon, as well as at the National Memorial for the Unborn in Tennessee. Darlene's eyes welled up with tears when she read the words inscribed on the plaque: "Please Forgive Us. We Love You. Your Mom And Dad."

"And people say it is no big deal," she softly spoke.

Thirty-three years later, the life I attempted so hard to conceal and forget has not only become a large part of who I am, but also plays a huge role in the work I am doing today. My abortion was, and still is, a *very* "big deal." If not for my Savior's tender mercies, it would all be far too much to bear.

Abby came to PRC with her mind set on abortion. She had a complete change of heart after being presented with the truth about her options. Abby had experienced two previous abortions and initially told me she was "fine" with both of them. But during her ultrasound she began to cry. Except for the briefest moment, she did not allow her eyes to rest on the screen. I asked Abby if this was hard for her. She nodded as tears slid down her cheeks. I asked if she would like me to stop the ultrasound procedure. She nodded again, and tears rushed harder.

I shut off the machine. Abby sat up and pulled her knees to her chest. She rocked back and forth, wailing loudly. Her cries, which seemed to come from the very depths of her being, could be heard throughout the building. I gave her a few moments, just standing beside her, feeling incredibly helpless. I quietly prayed for wisdom. *What should I do next?* I then asked her what she was thinking.

"This is how far along I was with my last abortion. If only I had known," she sobbed. Cold reality had hit hard when Abby saw her baby moving vigorously inside her.

I shared with Abby how I had found forgiveness and healing through Jesus Christ for my own abortion, and referred her to HEART. Abby has since given birth to a beautiful baby girl.

Another client expressed frustration with the abortion clinic she had gone to with a previous pregnancy. She had not been told anything about fetal development or anything of the possible harmful emotional or physical effects of abortion. She said that the abortion clinic had performed an ultrasound, but the technician had turned the screen away from her view.

On PRC's ultrasound exit interview, this hurting young woman wrote in response to this question: "What information did you gain from your ultrasound experience?"

"That it is a baby."

In response to that same question, another client wrote, "A lot! It is a human life."

Tara had undergone nine abortions and was planning to abort this new pregnancy, as well. Through grief-stricken eyes, she told me that she had never before been told the truth. That day Tara chose to give her baby life and left with adoption referrals. I later spoke with Tara, who told me she was carrying twins and was in the process of selecting adoptive parents for her babies. Several months later, Tara brought me a photograph of these dear babies, who are now living on the east coast with the family she chose for them.

One client wrote on her exit interview, "I am thankful the Pregnancy Resource Center is here to help women stop and think. The counsel I received made me stop and think, and as a result, I have decided not to have an abortion and to keep my baby. Thank you for helping me to stop and think."

Most women I have seen facing an untimely pregnancy are so consumed by fear and their emotions that it is difficult for them to stop and think clearly on their own. How well I remember being in that very same place! How I wish someone would have helped me to stop and think.

I saw a client first in the counseling room for a pregnancy test and then for an ultrasound. Hannah gave me all sorts of reasons why she felt abortion was her only option. For many of her reasons, I had experienced similar circumstances in my own life.

Hannah told me she had a seven-month-old baby at home. It would be "unrealistic" for her to be expected to have another baby so soon. I told her my son had been seven months old when I became pregnant with my daughter.

She told me she always wanted to be a registered nurse, but that if she had this baby she would be "way too old" to ever go to nursing school. She was twenty-eight years old. I told Hannah I was forty years old when I graduated from college as a registered nurse.

She told me she did not think she would have any difficulty living with an abortion. I told her that the following day would be the twenty-ninth anniversary of the abortion of my baby, and how that decision has been a huge regret. Hannah expressed surprise that I still remembered the date so many years later.

I told Hannah that the abortion of my baby had broken my heart, and how in Christ alone I found healing. I told her I now had the confidence that I would one day be reunited with my baby in heaven. She asked how I could be so certain I would one day be with my baby in heaven. I then shared the gospel with Hannah, who was Buddhist.

As Hannah stood up to leave the ultrasound room, she said, "Before coming to this clinic, I honestly thought that all that was inside of me was just a clump of blood. I did not know you were going to make me think. Now, I am going to have to think."

I offered Hannah a second ultrasound.

She replied that she would "think about it."

Five weeks later she telephoned the center and asked if the offer for a second ultrasound still stood. I was thrilled to hear she was still pregnant!

After Hannah's second ultrasound, and as she was walking out of the ultrasound room, she stopped. "I guess the reason I came back today was because I wanted you to tell me not to do it."

I knew the "it" Hannah was referring to was abortion. At PRC we never tell anybody not to have an abortion. We tell them the truth about their options. We hope and pray they will choose life for their babies, but we never tell them not to have an abortion.

But that day I looked into Hannah's pleading eyes and said, "Hannah, this is your choice to make, not mine. But if you are asking me to tell you not to do it, then I will tell you: Don't do it. Don't have an abortion. For me, abortion was not a quick and easy fix, but rather a very temporary Band-Aid. I can tell you that abortion hurts. I can tell you that abortion is not God's plan for you or your baby."

"Thank you," Hannah replied as her eyes filled with tears, "I just needed somebody to tell me not to do it."

Several weeks later, Hannah telephoned the center. She had just had an ultrasound with her doctor and was expecting a baby girl. She thanked me for doing the work I was doing and told me how helpful it had been for her. "Thanks for helping me see the truth. Thanks to you, I am going to be having my baby."

Hannah brought her daughter into the center for me to meet several months later. I know that it was not because of me that Hannah chose life for her baby. I know that it was—and always is—because of God, Who chose a flawed person like me to be one of His many vessels.

Chapter Fourteen

A FRIEND ONCE COMMENTED to me regarding her observation of the sharp contrast between the mindset of the culture in the United States and the mindset of her native country of Costa Rica.

"In my country, nobody has anything. Large, extended families live together under one roof in small, primitive homes, and everybody is happy. In this country (the U.S.), people have so much, but everybody is depressed and killing their babies. In my country nobody talks about there not being enough money or it not being the right time. The announcement of a pregnancy is always celebrated, regardless of the circumstances."

These statements are exaggerated on both sides, but there is an underlying truth in my friend's summation. It is a sad commentary on the state of things here in the United States.

During a Sunday school class I used to teach, the subject of abortion came up in a conversation between two girls.

The younger one, who was nine years old, asked what the word "abortion" meant.

Before I could decide how best to answer, the eleven-year-old girl said, "It means to kill a baby."

Out of the mouths of babes comes the simplicity of the truth! The thought of offending anyone never entered the girl's mind. In honest and simple terms, she spoke the truth: Abortion kills babies.

In my original draft of this section, I confronted Christians in general for not stepping out more on behalf of the unborn. I wrote how irreprehensible abortion is from any viewpoint and for any reason. I gave lots of statistics and thought I sounded quite convincing. But in my heart, I felt uneasy.

My daughter read the original draft and commented, "Mom, you need to come across a bit softer. Someone may read this, who feels just as strongly for a different cause, and feels led to place their energy there. A woman pregnant as a result of rape or incest may feel you don't sympathize with her plight."

Although my daughter is firmly pro-life, she perceived that I came across somewhat harsh and insensitive. I earnestly sought the Lord on this and sensed Him speaking to me these words: "*Just show them your heart.*"

So that is what I will do. I am not attempting to elicit sympathy or to place blame anywhere for my abortion other than precisely where it belongs—on me. I knew exactly what I was doing when I made that decision, and I take full responsibility. Just the same, that abortion broke my heart; that abortion killed my baby. I believe that each and every abortion breaks the Father-heart of God.

There are those who consider themselves pro-life but make exceptions in the instances of rape, incest, when an abnormality of the unborn baby exists, or when the life of the mother is at stake. These are the tough cases—gut-wrenching, agonizing, heart-breaking cases. It is easy for someone looking in from the outside to state their views. People have their own thoughts and are eager to express their opinions.

The real issue here is the sovereignty of God. The only view which should ultimately matter is what God has to say about the life of the unborn. God's Word should always be our moral guide, not fallible human logic. Some situations are just plain hard.

I have learned that God speaks truth to hearts and gives a sense of peace in making tough decisions when one truly seeks Him. I have also experienced the comfort only the Holy Spirit can bring, when everything seems overwhelming and hopeless.

I'd like to add that Jesus has mended my broken heart. He has tended to my broken baby and is keeping him safely in His care.

I believe God's heart is speaking to your heart and to mine, that His heart is running over with love: for you, for me, and for the woman who has been hurt so many times that her heart has grown cold. For the child who has been abused and betrayed. For the man standing on the street corner with no one to love. For the newborn left in a dumpster to die. For the young boy, holding out his cup and asking for but one penny. For the young woman who has sold herself in order to put food in her belly. For the old woman who has forgotten her name, and who does not recognize the face of the love of her life. For the mom who has just learned her soldier son has died. For the father who must struggle to explain to his young children why Jesus took their mama to heaven. For the wife who feels all alone. For the teenager who does not feel he fits in anywhere, and who would rather be dead. For the husband who feels misunderstood. For the pastor who is weary. For the old man who has suddenly lost the wife of his youth. For the businessman who has lost everything. For the spouse who has strayed or who has been betrayed.

And for the tiny, unborn baby, who is stretching and growing, eagerly anticipating all that life has in store, who suddenly in terror is retracting from the vacuum or the knife or the saline, crying out with all his might, "Mama! Aren't you going to help me?"

As Christians, we need to ask God what He would have us do. We cannot say we do not know about the thousands of helpless babies who are being slaughtered daily in this country, because we *do* know. Proverbs 24:11-12 tells us that we will be held accountable for what we knew: "Rescue those being led away to death; hold back those staggering towards slaughter. If you say, 'But we knew nothing about this,' does not He who weighs the heart perceive it? Does not He who guards your life know it? Will He not repay each person according to what he has done?"

Jesus loves every boy and girl, every **man** and woman, every little baby—born or unborn—in this whole, wide world. They are all precious in His sight. He does not view any person or any situation as being hopeless of His redemptive power. If He did, I certainly would not be where I am today.

I believe God's heart is crying out to all who will listen that He is taller than the highest mountain, smarter than the intelligence of any man, braver than the mightiest warrior, and broader than the widest sea. There is nothing you or I may go through that will catch Him off-guard or unaware. He is all-knowing, all-seeing, and all-delivering. He can turn the bleakest and darkest circumstance into the most promising and joyous tomorrow. His power is insurmountable and His love inescapable.

Chapter Fifteen

I AM OFTEN HUMBLED when I am reminded of how far the Lord has brought me and how far I still have to go. It seems I require frequent reminders of where I have been, the choices I have made, and the thoughts I have entertained.

Once, following an ultrasound, I went to pick out a baby quilt to give to my client. I stood there pondering which quilt to give her. She was dirty and smelled badly. One quilt was especially exquisite and special. *I shouldn't give her this one*, I thought. *Her baby will probably be dirty and smelly too.*

As quickly as the thought came, the Holy Spirit rebuked me. *"Is this one any less worthy?"*

"Of course not," I muttered, ashamed, and handed her the especially nice quilt.

Heather's eyes moistened. "Thank you. It is so beautiful." She smiled and hugged it closely to her face.

Months later, Heather returned to the center to show off her baby boy. "The quilt really helped me make up my mind to keep my son. I clung to it for weeks while I slept, crying and scared. I am so thankful I did not have an abortion. I love my son more than I ever thought I could love anybody."

Many of PRC's supporters faithfully provide baby blankets, hats, and other baby needs. Offering something tangible to these ladies who have chosen life for their baby helps to cement that decision.

In certain circumstances, even some Christians feel an abortion is preferable to life. There are times when I have felt torn when one of my ultrasound mothers chooses life for her baby. Joy, but also concern for the future I foresee for that young one. At these times, the Lord reminds me that He has a specific purpose for every human life; that every human being is His workmanship and bears His image.

I typically present the idea of adoption in situations where I perceive the woman sitting before me is of questionable mothering material. Several of my clients have chosen adoption. More often than not, however, adoption is not an option they will even consider.

I know of two of my ultrasound clients' babies who have been placed into foster care, due to abuse. When I hear about such situations, I cannot help but feel discouraged. It is at these times when God faithfully reaffirms to my heart that regardless of the outcome, standing for life is always the right thing to do. It is what He requires of us. "This day I call heaven and earth as witnesses against you, that I have set before you life and death, blessings and curses. Now choose life, so that you and your children may live and that you may love the Lord your God, listen to His voice and hold fast to Him" (Deuteronomy 30:19-20).

Maria told me she was looking for a church. I invited her to visit ours. She soon began attending regularly. Life for Maria had been riddled with hard blows from the start. Her coping mechanism was to shut herself off from anyone who tried to get too close. Maria had been hurt so many times that she was afraid of trusting anyone. As a result, she had stopped allowing herself to feel much of anything.

At Maria's request, I experienced the thrill of being her birth coach. I cannot adequately put into words the exhilaration of cheering a young one into this world for whose life I had fought so hard, for one who might very well have never made it here.

When Maria tested positive for pregnancy, her doctor handed her the telephone number for Planned Parenthood, advising she have an abortion. Maria's doctor told her that he believed she was ill-equipped both emotionally and psychologically to parent. Maria came to PRC because the day she telephoned Planned Parenthood they were closed. She was looking for someone to talk to regarding her pregnancy. She spent time with one of PRC's counselors, who then referred her for an ultrasound.

Soon after the birth of Maria's baby boy, she asked our pastor and his wife to adopt him, acknowledging that she felt incapable of giving him what she knew he deserved. Days after the initial steps were taken in the adoption process, the entire proceedings went haywire. Maria had changed her mind.

Feeling terribly disappointed and sad, I literally became sick because of how things had turned so upside down. Maria's life was incredibly unstable, and she had already proven to be an unfit mother. I hurt for her little one. I hurt for our pastor and his family, especially for his wife, Betty, as she had grown very attached to this baby boy.

In the midst of the legal process of returning the baby to Maria's custody, Betty gave me a gift she had handmade, a framed, intricately detailed Scripture verse she had painted, from Ephesians 2:10: "For we are His workmanship, created in Christ Jesus to do good works, which God has prepared in advance for us to do." Included was a sweet note of encouragement, saying she was praying I wouldn't become discouraged in the work I was doing with the Pregnancy Resource Centers.

Betty telephoned the morning after the adoption process was turned about and read to me another Bible verse she believed came from the Lord to encourage me. I was deeply moved by how Betty reached out to me in the midst of her own pain.

Not long after Maria's baby was returned to her custody, the state removed him, due to child endangerment and neglect. After all was said and done, I was emotionally drained. One morning near the end of this ordeal, I telephoned Diana, my then nurse manager, and told her I felt spent, with nothing left to give. Diana suggested I stay home from work that day and rest in the Lord. I did, and I was refueled as only He can do.

Chapter Sixteen

IT TAKES EFFORT to remain fixed on the Lord; a conscious choice to do so. When I get lazy, I invariably find myself off course, entangled in unbecoming thoughts and actions; wallowing right back in my own self pity; whining that nothing feels right. Just about the time I determine that all is miserable, the Holy Spirit mercifully convicts me that I have brought it upon myself by pushing Him aside. He reminds me that He must be first and I last. There is no other way.

Time and time again clients professing to be Christians display no indication of being anything but comfortable with their immoral lifestyles. Three out of four of the Pregnancy Resource Center's clients profess to be Christians. How easily I find myself feeling self-righteous. I am reproved by the Holy Spirit every time.

God's Word states that compared to His perfect holiness, even our righteous acts are as filthy rags. With God as the standard, we all fall miserably short of hitting the mark. If not for the grace accomplished on the cross, not one of us would stand the slightest chance.

After spending time with a client who was particularly exasperating in her self-indulgent attitude, I sighed. "Lord, when will these girls get it together?"

I clearly heard God respond to my heart, "*When will you?*"

As mature Christians, our struggles may be disguised in neat, tidy packages and less obvious on the outside, but God is all-knowing. How many times have we let Him down? How many times has He forgiven us for the same old thing?

"I could *never* carry my baby for nine months and then give it away," clients typically respond when adoption is presented as an option worth considering.

But you can kill it has crossed my mind more often than not.

"*You thought the exact same thing,*" the Holy Spirit gently reproofs.

My heart immediately softens toward the young woman whom I know is scared and feeling pressed into a corner—with abortion seeming the only reasonable solution.

Sophie expressed regret over a past abortion and described her experience with the abortion clinic:

"They pressured and pressured until I caved. They kept asking, 'Do you have any idea how hard it is going to be to be a mom so young? How expensive it will be? How it is going to ruin your life? You are only nineteen years old and not married. This would not be fair to the baby. How can you even consider having a baby right now?'"

Sophie had been four months pregnant at the time and shared with me how deeply she resents that abortion clinic, and how disappointed she is in herself for "not being stronger; for giving in."

As I listened, I felt anger toward those responsible for such pressure, and I felt real sadness for Sophie. Then the stark realization hit me: The farther along one is in her pregnancy, the higher the revenue for the abortion clinic. I am sure that at four months of pregnancy, the rate is steep.

Many of these young women have not been raised with any religious beliefs whatsoever. Oftentimes, from early on they have been taught that a woman should have the right to choose. Frequently it is the parents pressuring their daughter to abort.

It is not uncommon for the boyfriend, who is also often terrified, to plead that abortion would be best for all. I hear this statement often:

"My boyfriend will break up with me if I keep this baby."

The cold truth is that when abortion occurs to spare a relationship, it typically does just the opposite. The woman who aborts her baby to keep her boyfriend often grows to resent and want to rid herself of the man she sacrificed her child for, ultimately blaming him for the ending of her baby's life.

The girlfriends of these young women, who have oftentimes themselves been groomed into believing abortion is sometimes the most humane decision, frequently counsel their pregnant friend that she would be foolish, even selfish, to have a baby right now.

Having personally experienced an unwanted pregnancy, I can relate. My heart hurts for these young women as I recognize the pain and fear in their eyes. I understand that for where they are in their life, abortion seems the only solution. I know how difficult it can be to see beyond today and the seemingly overwhelming circumstances of right now.

I know firsthand how scary and hard it all can be, but I also know how utterly heart ripping the effects of abortion can be. I have the amazing privilege of being able to encourage these dear ladies toward Jesus, the only One who holds all the answers; the only One who can meet all of their needs if they will but trust Him.

One mother sat alongside her daughter, insisting abortion was the only answer. Her daughter said nothing. She sat there crying, her shoulders shaking inconsolably. I expressed my empathy to the mother, telling her that as a mother myself, I understood her pain. At the same time, I suggested she allow her daughter to make her own decision regarding her pregnancy, as she would be the one most impacted by whatever decision was made.

At first, this mother watched guardedly as her well-formed grandbaby squirmed about on the ultrasound screen. Then, as if a switch had been flipped, her expression grew dim. She took her daughter's hand and broke down into heart-wrenching sobs. The choice of life was made that afternoon, and this mother chose to lovingly support her daughter in that decision. Sadly, the unborn baby died several weeks later, due to unforeseen complications. But thankfully, the baby's mother can live with the peace that she did the best she could to give her baby life; and both hearts—mother and daughter—have been changed regarding the unborn.

I spent time with another young woman who was heart-broken because of a past abortion. From the moment Laura sat in the chair next to mine until she left the ultrasound room, tears streamed down her face. I shared my own story with Laura, telling her of the love and healing to be found in Jesus Christ. I asked her if she knew Him.

"No," she replied, shaking her head.

"Would you like to?" I asked.

"Yes," she nodded. Fresh tears gushed.

Laura prayed aloud, unashamedly broken, as she gave her heart to Jesus. I explained to her how her new commitment to Christ would include making some tough life-style changes, such as sexual purity until marriage. She was incredibly open.

We then began the ultrasound procedure. On that screen appeared a perfectly formed baby, with no detectable heartbeat. We prayed together and scheduled a follow-up ultrasound. When Laura returned for her next appointment, she told me through a radiant smile, "I have experienced peace and joy this past week like I never have before."

On the ultrasound screen it was apparent her baby's size had not changed. There was still no detectable heartbeat. God had carried this baby to heaven prior to the first ultrasound. He had arranged the ultrasound appointment because of His great love for this baby's mama. He had prepared and ripened her heart to be ready that day to receive His Son as her Savior and to find hope in regards to her past abortion.

With another client's ultrasound I was again unable to identify a heartbeat. Audrey telephoned the center one week later, informing the receptionist she had miscarried and requested that I call her.

When I returned her call, I was moved by how this same woman, who only one week earlier had desperately wanted to end her baby's life, was now grieving over the loss of that same baby. With the exception of just one client, I have seen this same response over and over. This demonstrates to me that our hearts recognize the truth, in spite of how hard we try to hide from that truth. A mama's heart is just that. Losing a child under any circumstance hurts.

Chapter Seventeen

THE ONE SITUATION in my work with PRC that has probably touched me the deepest, which moved my heart to nearly breaking, was witnessing the heartbreak of a father.

Sam first came to the center with his girlfriend, Kate, for a pregnancy test. Later, they returned for an ultrasound. Sam was unusually conscientious for his young age and seemed so sincere. In the counseling room, with Kate's PRC counselor as a witness, Sam—down on one knee—asked Kate to marry him. He promised to protect her and their young one for life. Kate only stared flatly at him in response.

During my pre-ultrasound counseling with Kate, and then during the ultrasound itself, Kate had erected an almost visible wall between her heart and the truth. She did ask me one gripping question, which was about the only point where I saw any depth of emotion.

"If I continue with this pregnancy, how will my child feel someday if I tell him or her, 'I almost aborted you'? How will that make my child feel?"

I replied, "I wish I could look into my child's eyes today and say, 'I almost aborted you, and I am so thankful I didn't.' I would give almost anything to be able to say that."

Kate's eyes filled with tears at this, and she sighed deeply. I dared to hope that her "wall" had crumbled. But at the very end of our time together, as she was heading toward the door, she paused and asked, "Can you tell me where the nearest abortion clinic is?"

My heart sank. "No, I cannot."

"Why not?"

"Because I believe abortion is harmful to women and to babies. In all good conscience, I cannot give you that information."

Kate nodded as if to say, *I know; I understand.*

When she left the building, I locked myself in the ultrasound room and cried out, "Almighty God, spare this baby."

I was sitting at the front desk several weeks later when Sam walked into the center alone. His eyes met mine, and he began to cry. He informed me that Kate had gone ahead with an abortion.

"Is there anybody who can help me through this?" he implored.

I felt heartsick. It is always painful to learn one of these babies has been aborted, especially when I have often watched them squirm about on the ultrasound screen only days before. But seeing this father's heart so broken was especially painful. There stood this tall, burly young man, shamelessly grieving for his child. I don't know if I will ever forget those eyes—those sad, tear-filled eyes.

I felt inadequate. All I could do was tell Sam how sorry I was. I stood there and cried with him. I also gave Sam a referral to PRC's post-abortion support group for men, along with a book authored by Pastor Jack Hayford titled,

I'll Hold You in Heaven. I told him what a comfort this book had been for me.

Terri, one of the center's staff, telephoned me at home a month later to tell me Sam had come back to the center to thank me. He had also left me a bouquet of flowers.

The next day, while I was with an ultrasound client, Sam returned to the center. He waited for quite some time until I was finished.

"I just wanted to thank you in person," he told me. "Although the outcome did not go as we had hoped, you really made a big difference for me." Sam added that prior to Kate's ultrasound he had been primarily concerned with maintaining his relationship with her. "I was willing to support her in whatever decision she made in order to hold on to her. But seeing that ultrasound changed everything. It gave me an entirely different perspective."

Sam also said that he had looked into the post-abortion healing group and he had been "re-evaluating" his walk with God. "I've been going to church again the past couple of weeks. I'm seriously relooking at my life, and at some of the choices I've made. I broke off my relationship with Kate and changed my phone number and e-mail address so she can't contact me. I have to move on."

What an encouragement this was for me! It is rare to see one of the boyfriends return to the centers alone, seeking support. And then to come *again* to say thank you? Well, I doubt I will ever experience that again.

Chapter Eighteen

THERE WAS ONE point when I had seen a slew of difficult clients, which left me unusually weary. Disheartened, I once again began to question if I was making much of a difference—or even a dent—in these hard hearts.

I learned later that two of these clients went through with their initial plans to abort, even after they had seen their active babies on the ultrasound screen. Both had aborted previous pregnancies. For one it had only been six months earlier, at twenty weeks of pregnancy. For the other, who at the time was twenty-three years old, this would be her eighth abortion.

Another client refused to look at the ultrasound screen, shielding her eyes with her hands the entire time. When I showed her the pictures of her baby, her face was void of expression. Her eyes were vacant as she said to me, "I feel numb, and our time together has made absolutely no difference in how I feel toward the fetus."

Another woman, during the course of our pre-ultrasound counseling, suddenly glared at me and said, "I know what you guys are all about."

On her post-ultrasound exit interview she wrote "abortion" in response to the question asking what her intentions now were for her pregnancy. As she walked out of the center, she slung the brochures and ultrasound pictures I had given her across the counter of the receptionist's desk.

I realized this was not a personal assault, but it still felt like I had been slapped in the face. I had just returned from a restful vacation with my husband. I was feeling rejuvenated and ready to give my all to this work. Then right off the bat, with my very first ultrasound client, my first day back to work, I got shot down. I felt discouraged! Here I was, back in the trenches and being reminded of the ups and downs of this intense battle for life. I found myself entertaining thoughts about how much easier another nursing job would be, one free from all these heartfelt challenges and the constant emotional roller-coaster ride.

As I wrestled with these thoughts, God spoke to my heart: "If you guys weren't there, where else would they go?"

I knew immediately where they would go—to one of the many abortion clinics in the area. If PRC and other similar ministries were not available, there would be a lot fewer women hearing about the hope to be found in Jesus, and there would be many more babies aborted.

There are women who return repeatedly to PRC for pregnancy tests, demonstrating little—if any—evidence of change in their lives. Over and over I am reminded of how dark and sinful this world is. There are still times I find myself shocked and oftentimes saddened by the stories I hear.

Jeanie had so much more going for her in life compared with many of the women PRC sees. She was in her early thirties, had a great job, which provided full medical coverage, and had recently purchased a home. She also had the benefit of a strong support network of family and friends living nearby.

The complicated part for Jeanie was that the father of her baby was a long-time friend. She did not foresee there ever being anything more between them. They had celebrated New Year's Eve, had drunk too much alcohol, and subsequently slept together—something they had never done before. He had been visiting from out of state and had already flown back home.

The ultrasound screen showed a squirming, well-developed baby of fourteen weeks. Tears filled Jeanie's eyes as her hand lightly brushed the screen. "It looks like it's just you and me, kid."

Jeanie had arrived for her ultrasound appointment feeling overwhelmed and inept; she left professing confidence in her ability to parent. She had even signed up for PRC's parenting class. In the weeks following Jeanie's ultrasound, I was unable to reach her by telephone. Then late one afternoon, Jeanie called the center and asked to speak with me:

"I just couldn't go through with it," she said, sounding crushed.

When I asked Jeanie what she meant, she replied that she had gone ahead with an abortion at nineteen weeks of pregnancy. "You were the first person I thought to call," she continued, her voice shaking.

"How are you doing?" I asked.

"Terribly. I feel so sad."

She was reaching out to me for comfort, and I had to endeavor to be strong in return. Within, it felt as though my own heart had been ripped out. As we spoke, I envisioned her baby twisting and turning on the ultrasound screen only a few weeks before. I did my best to encourage Jeanie and referred her to HEART. I told her she could call or drop in the center anytime she needed to talk. After we said goodbye, I hung up the telephone. I then closed the door to the ultrasound room, dropped my head, and wept. I sat there for a long time crying out to God, and then I telephoned Diana, just to unload. She prayed with me.

God has taught me that He is not asking me to change these young women's hearts or minds. I am not capable of doing that. He only asks for obedience to His call. None of us are responsible for the choices another makes. It is the Holy Spirit who realigns hearts and attitudes. It is He who does the softening. It is He Who speaks truth to hurting hearts.

While I know this is true, I still struggle. I want to say just the right words that will make the woman who is so out of sync with God's way of thinking transform her thoughts to line up with His. At these times, God is faithful to remind me that I am merely a vessel He has chosen to work through. Recognizing—and more importantly—accepting this makes it much easier to press on. I am grateful to serve a God who is willing to carry the load for me. I know I must leave it with Him. Otherwise, it becomes way too heavy.

There are times when it seems that nothing I say makes an impact. The woman sitting in front of me is there solely for the free pregnancy test and is not open to making any changes in her life.

One such client confided that she was dating a member of a prominent gang in Portland. I held her sweet baby boy while she used the bathroom. As he rested quietly in my arms, I cuddled his head into my neck, placed my hand on his back, and prayed for the cycle of godlessness to be broken with him. I prayed for God's grace and covering to be realized in this little one's life, that he would come to know the Lord at an early age, and that he would have a heart that was steadfast after God.

I may not have made a difference that day in his mama's life, but I could pray for this baby and in faith believe this would make a difference in *his* life. Who knows? He may be the one to someday lead his mama to Jesus.

Chapter Nineteen

A WAR IS RAGING between life and death, with soldiers staunchly posted on both sides of the battle line. This is not a war between people, groups, or political parties, however. This is a spiritual battle. But greater is He that is in us than He that is in the world (1 John 4:4).

There have been various and ongoing attacks against the ministry of PRC. Centers have been defaced and vandalized. It is tempting at times to believe the enemy is unbeatable, that this war is unwinnable. There are days when the battle line between life and death seems impossible to cross over. It becomes easy to feel trampled and defeated. Yet in spite of the downfalls, there have been many victories in this battle for life. And if only one baby's life is saved or only one woman comes to Jesus through the work that is being done, then it has been worth it all. Thank God, there have been so many more than just one!

The changes taking place in these women often show a domino effect as attitudes toward abortion are altered in the hearts of their boyfriends, peers, and parents. Only God knows the full effect as others witness these changes and are also altered.

We at PRC don't always see the fruits of our labor, and the enemy, Satan, gets great pleasure from our discouragement. He constantly lurks about, watching and waiting for an opportunity to pounce; whispering words of doubt every chance he gets.

The enemy sometimes catches me off guard, but I find that the more I am tuned into God, the less successful Satan is in bringing me down. The more I look to God's Word, and the more that I call upon His name, the less ground the enemy gains. The more filled up I am with Jesus and determined to stand firm in Christ ahead of time, the less of an impact the enemy makes.

I have learned to have the mindset that although what I am presently going through may not make sense, and although I may not understand it, I will choose to trust God anyway. This is definitely a struggle, because it is far more natural for me to stew and fret.

As I was writing this section about choosing to trust God in spite of circumstances, the sincerity of my words was put to the test. I was typing away when my dad telephoned and told me that my oldest brother, Gary, had been diagnosed with esophageal cancer. What a blow! Hearing that Gary had cancer was really hard.

Thank God for modern, medical technology! The surgeons were able to remove his entire esophagus and rebuild it with part of his stomach. Gary has gone through a long and difficult recovery, but today he is doing well. He is the first to give God all the glory.

Another time when it was difficult for me to wholly trust God was when my beloved aunt, my dad's sister, was diagnosed with leukemia. Within eight weeks of receiving that diagnosis, she went home to be with Jesus. Her illness came on suddenly, and her health declined rapidly. It was unexpected and a real shock for the entire family.

My aunt and I had always been close. However, her son's betrayal of my daughter, and my aunt's discovery of her husband's betrayal of me reshaped our relationship. After learning of my daughter's sexual abuse by my cousin, we no longer visited my aunt at her home. Although my aunt was saddened by all that had happened and the changes that had occurred as a result, she still had an unyielding loyalty to her son. She'd hoped everything could be as it was before, but that was no longer possible.

After Jerry, our children, and I moved to Oregon, my aunt and I stayed in touch. She even visited us a few times, but there was always a hint of strain between us. I am glad I flew down to Southern California to spend a few days with her after she became so sick. Shortly afterwards, I returned with my parents for her funeral. My aunt's death was a huge loss for me, and I still miss her. At the same time, I rejoice that she is with Jesus, happy and at peace.

Chapter Twenty

INOT ONLY HAVE the privilege of serving at PRC, but I am richly served as well. My faith is strengthened whenever I observe God making a way where there appears to *be* no conceivable way. Answered prayers and changed hearts elevate my confidence in Him. I am both stretched and humbled as He shows me time and time again how highly He regards those considered by man as unworthy. Such as the clients I see who are dirty, homeless, prostitutes, mentally challenged, drug addicts, gang members…and the babies they are carrying. Through my work with PRC, I have gained a greater appreciation and respect for every human life.

It is such a blessing to work in a Christian environment, where each day begins with prayer, and where there is such a common bond between the center's workers.

Following an ultrasound session with an unusually bitter and hardened young woman, I felt emotionally depleted. After this client left the center, Bethany, one of the center's volunteers, told me she had been praying for me and for my client throughout our time together. What an encouragement and blessing!

After a period of rest, I experienced a long, drawn-out period of obvious attacks by the enemy. One evening after work, I pulled up our driveway and parked in my usual spot. I opened the door and got out of the car. With my first step, it felt as though my foot had come up against a wall. I literally felt a solid barrier. I fell hard onto the pavement, flat on my face. I lay there stunned, looking around for an explanation. There was none. My glasses had shattered with the impact. One of my cheeks stung, and I felt a slight trickle of blood.

The next day, I turned the steering wheel in the direction of the center median to turn into the PRC parking lot for work. Then I watched helplessly as a car sped toward my side of the car. The driver was staring straight at me! Why this car did not slam into me can only be accredited to the grace of God.

I was walking along the sidewalk a couple of days later, headed to a different PRC, when a woman wearing dark-colored pants and a dark, hooded jacket looked intently into my eyes. She said in a hushed voice as she briskly passed, "We know who you are."

A short time later, while walking along that same sidewalk, I suddenly tripped and fell, scraping my nose and one of my cheeks. I might have chalked this up to clumsiness, but all of these incidents occurred so close together that it made it difficult for me to dismiss them as mere ineptness.

Next, I groped through a dismal period of depression. I looked for a reason, as I had not struggled with prolonged depression since before going through HEART. But I could find no legitimate reason for how I felt. Typically, the times I feel sad come as a result of a particular circumstance. As a rule, I am able to put my finger on the source, and the sadness is short-lived. However, this unexplained gloominess persisted for weeks and I didn't know why.

During this same time period, two PRC clients—one right after the other—stood up and yelled at me. I have never experienced such a response from a client before or since. The first woman sat in a chair in the counseling room, smiling serenely. She then suddenly stood, pointed her index finger at my face, and announced, "I am getting really bad vibes from you."

Just as suddenly, she regained her composure and sat back down. I asked her what I had done or said to offend her. "Oh, nothing at all," she replied. "Don't mind me."

She was extremely abortion-minded, so I offered her an ultrasound, to which she agreed. She followed me downstairs to the front desk, where the ultrasound appointment book is kept. As I began to flip through the pages, her eyes glazed over and her demeanor stiffened. She muttered something about "not needing the stupid ultrasound" then turned sharply and hurried out the front door.

The second woman suddenly stood and glared at me. "Are you willing to buy diapers, formula and pay for childcare for my baby? If you're not, then you have no business talking to me about the physical and emotional risks involved with abortion. I'll take my chances." She then sat back down and her tears began to flow. I shared with her my own abortion story and told her I understood that this was a really hard decision. We talked for a lengthy time about the truth regarding each of her pregnancy options. By the end of our time together she apologized to me for her angry outburst and thanked me for taking the time to talk with her. I have had no contact with this young woman since and have no idea what decision she ultimately made as to the outcome of her pregnancy. But I do know her heart was softened.

God brought me through all of this. He could have prevented it altogether, but He didn't. I believe he didn't prevent it because He was at work, refining and growing me in Him.

During these times (when I was actually paying attention rather than wallowing in self pity) I sensed God's presence and power. It was so real, and His love and peace transcended everything. I suspect this present reprieve is temporary and that once again it will be a struggle to hold on to Him. John 16:33 says: "… in the world you will have tribulation …" But that verse also carries Jesus' promise "… but be of good cheer, for I have overcome the world" (NKJ).

This life-journey is a battle. Just about the time it seems I have made headway, sure enough—here comes the unexpected! Here comes another battle. Yet it is during the especially hard times I rediscover the all-satiating joy that I can find only in Him.

And that rediscovery makes it all worthwhile.

During one of these struggles, a friend reminded me of the strength found in Proverbs 18:10: "The name of the Lord is a strong tower. The righteous run to it and are safe."

The name of my Lord is my strong tower. When I run to Him, I am safe. It is when I rely on my own strength rather than on His that I am miserable. Then the enemy makes headway. It is when I remove my eyes from my Lord that I fumble and lose my joy. Through it all—the good times and the bad—I have come to realize I can bear the pain of losing anything, as long as I never lose Jesus. He is my reason, my strength, and my all.

I wrestled through a time of disillusionment after learning someone I highly esteemed was a fallible human being, just like the rest of us. While pouring my heart out to the Lord about this, He flooded me with the warmth of His presence and showed me a delightful mental image: I saw a long, narrow, dusty road leading to a glistening, golden, jewel-encrusted gate. In my spirit, I sensed God admonishing me that I must let go of those negative feelings. Instead, I must fix my eyes on the goal, on the finish line. There isn't enough room on the narrow road to look to the right or to the left. If I do, I will lose my balance and fall. I must look straight ahead to that golden gate. He reminded me of the mercy He has and continues to graciously impart to me.

God in His goodness sends along the perk I need, just when I need it most. I am convinced He finds great delight in sending an embrace His children's way. A client will bring her baby into the center for me to meet when I most seem to need encouraging. Those moments lift my spirit more than anything else. What a delight it is to hold one of these babies in my arms, rejoicing in the victory that has been won! I keep a camera handy in the ultrasound room for these moments, and a photo album in my bedside drawer. I pull the album out when I need a pick-me-up.

Throughout her ultrasound, one client showed no change in her feeling toward her baby. Her arms remained tightly folded across her chest the entire time she sat next to me. During the ultrasound itself, she displayed no expression or emotion whatsoever. Her eyes appeared cold and hard. Not once did a trace of a smile cross her face.

I felt dismayed when she left, as if our time together had been pointless. Then one afternoon several months later,

I caught a glimpse of her as she passed by the ultrasound room. She was following a counselor into the maternity clothes room. Her tummy was bulging! Eagerly, I went to greet her. "What changed your mind?"

"I thought about everything you said after I left the ultrasound, and I just couldn't go through with the abortion."

As she spoke, her eyes shone and a huge smile covered her pretty face. What a gift from God that she came into the center on a day when I was there!

Another time, a couple came in, asking for me. When I came downstairs to greet them, Lily proudly thrust out her left hand, showing off a sparkling diamond ring. She was obviously with child. Both Lily's and Brian's faces glowed.

A few months earlier I had spent time with this couple in one of the counseling rooms. Brian had slumped in his chair the entire time, staring at me blankly with stone-cold eyes. During that session, Lily and Brian detailed to me all the reasons they could not have this baby. Lily had been accepted into a prestigious school in New York; Brian was in graduate school, also out of state.

I felt tremendously inept, and inwardly I asked God, *How in the world did I ever get into this situation or job, anyway? There are many others who are so much more articulate, so much more confident than I. Why me, Lord? You are going to have to help me out here, because counseling couples is definitely not my forte. Besides, since when am I an expert in counseling men? This is not fair, Lord.*

I struggled against the urge to hurry to my car, drive home, and hide out from all the intense emotion; to escape the need to always say the right thing, or even worse—the fear of saying the *wrong* thing.

"*I will give you the words to speak. Just relax and trust me,*" God patiently prodded.

Brian, Lily, and I spent the next two and a half hours talking. Once again, God lovingly reaffirmed that I can trust Him.

When they walked out of the center that day, I was not sure how much they had taken to heart or if they were going to allow their baby to live. I had offered them an ultrasound, to which they had responded, "We'll think about it."

After they left, I stopped and prayed, then faxed a prayer request to the PRC prayer chain. I then left it with the Lord, realizing that I did not have the power in and of myself to change anything.

Now, months later, they were standing in front of me, a testimony that our time together had not been in vain. Not only had they gotten married, but Lily had moved out of state to be with Brian while he completed graduate school. Lily had decided that having an intact family for her baby was most important.

"I can go back to school later like you did," she cheerfully said.

She *had* been listening. I had made a difference! They were completely different from the people I had met those many months before. The turnaround in these two was unbelievable. God had obviously worked a miracle in their hearts.

Another blessing came through a client named Jill, who walked into the center late one rainy afternoon. Jill approached the front desk and requested the abortion pill, RU486, which PRC does not provide. After talking with Jill for a while, Sally, the Center Director, asked if I would mind taking Jill's blood pressure. Jill's doctor had discontinued her blood pressure medication due to her pregnancy, and Jill was concerned her blood pressure might be getting too high.

I agreed to see Jill, and Sally escorted her upstairs to the ultrasound room. Jill looked completely worn out when she walked into the room. I asked her how she was doing.

"I'm tired, very tired." Jill sighed and plopped down into the chair next to my desk. Her blood pressure read normal. Jill spent the next hour and a half pouring her heart out to me.

It turned out that Jill had already seen a PRC counselor for a pregnancy test and was scheduled to see me for an ultrasound in two weeks. This day, however, she had decided to "just get things over with" and had returned to the center for RU486. I found this quite interesting because at this point she must have known that PRC does not provide this service. Again, it appeared God was orchestrating everything.

Jill told me she had nowhere to sleep that night other than at a man's house, whom she had recently met at a park. She had already slept several nights at his house, and he had asked for $200.00 a month for rent. When she told him she couldn't pay, he had responded, "We can work something out," and then had crawled into bed with her each night.

As Jill spoke, her tears never stopped. I told her of her great worth in Christ and how highly He values her.

Jill's voice quivered. "Why would that be? I'm the poster girl for damaged goods." She had a severe head cold and sat there sneezing, coughing, and crying. She told me about her mother, who had been a practicing witch with a black-magic religion since before Jill was born. "My mother has despised me from the beginning."

Jill added that she did not have close ties with her father, and her stepmother wanted nothing to do with her. Jill confessed that she had accepted Jesus Christ as her Savior "eons ago," but she had grown disillusioned. "The

Christians I know are not very forgiving. They put on a good show, but shun you in the end."

I was troubled. I wondered if I had ever been guilty of such un-Christ-like behavior, even subtly. I suspected that I had. I asked Jill if I could pray for her. She nodded and cried as I prayed out loud.

"Thank you," she said. "That was nice. It has been a long time since anyone prayed for me."

I brought PRC's referral box to the ultrasound room. Jill sat at my desk and made phone call after phone call until she was able to get into a shelter that very night. She also spoke with directors from two different maternity homes. One had an opening and arranged to meet with Jill the following afternoon.

Jill left PRC that afternoon with a total change of heart toward her baby. Now she had hope. God does not always work in the ways we expect, but He always *does* work. The encounter with Jill had begun with the casual act of taking her blood pressure.

Jill kept her ultrasound appointment two weeks later. She is presently enrolled in nursing school, raising her young daughter, and is actively involved in a church family.

I never imagined God would use me in the way He is, and I'm sure no one who knows me imagined it, either. All those years ago, when my brother Doug told me that God would someday use me in a ministry for grieving women, I was baffled. I had no knowledge of the existence of such a ministry. To be perfectly honest, ministering to women at *any* level intimidated me and held no appeal. Yet I never doubted that God planned to use me in *some* kind of ministry eventually. He had made that quite plain to my heart all along.

I always knew He had a plan, but for the longest time I had no curiosity as to what that plan might be. I was content to be a stay-at-home-mom and—up until my children were in middle school—had no desire to be anything else. And then the only desire I felt was to be a nurse.

It was not until I received the word from the Lord through Mary at church that Sunday morning, confirming the word He had spoken through my brother Doug sixteen years before, that I gave it much thought. I had been too preoccupied with the selfishness and the busyness of my own little world. That's what makes it all so amazing and all the more humbling, and so undeniably God.

Chapter Twenty-One

WHEN I WAS initially hired by PRC, I kept the nursing home job I already held, working for the nursing home every other weekend for over one year. Prior to PRC, I was on staff with a medical staffing agency as a "substitute nurse" and filled in at nearly every hospital in the greater Portland area. I was also employed with one hospital as well as with two different nursing homes. I believe God had me experience different areas of nursing so that I don't feel like I am missing anything now; and so that I can see the stark contrast between working in the world and working in a Christian environment.

In my previous nursing positions, God's name was mostly spoken as profanity. There were Christians at my other jobs, but we were always greatly outnumbered.

At one job I was pegged as the "goodie-two-shoes Christian." Certain co-workers seemed to go out of their way to berate me for my views. I was accused of being a prude for declining invitations to go out for a drink, or to a male-strip club with my peers after work. I found it startling how even the married nurses joined in. My disinterest clearly flustered them, and my moral views were seen as from another planet. Any attempts to share Christ were shunned.

But God did bless me with witnessing opportunities with several patients. He has also convicted me of the "open doors" of opportunity I walked right by when—due to my own self-interest—I desired to be accepted rather than be pegged as a fool.

One morning I was assigned a pre-op patient who was unusually frightened. Most people are apprehensive prior to surgery, but this woman was especially uneasy. Sensing the Holy Spirit's prompting, I asked her what she was so afraid of.

"Of dying," she answered.

"What is it about dying that frightens you?"

"Not knowing where I will go."

Talk about an open door! I shared with her the hope of eternal life in Jesus. She listened closely. Then without any apparent hesitation, she prayed out loud to invite Jesus into her heart. I never saw this woman again. By the time she returned to the unit, my shift had ended. I do not remember her name nor would I recognize her face. However, I believe that when our eyes meet in Heaven, we will know one another. What a delightful reunion that will be!

When I worked in a Jewish nursing home, I had the honor and pleasure of seeing an elderly woman acknowledge Jesus Christ, Y'shua, as her Messiah. Another woman brushed my hand as I told her of Jesus' love. She was dying, extremely lethargic, and unable to speak. Not more than ten minutes after I left her room, she breathed her last breath.

One afternoon I became engaged in a remarkable conversation with a woman in her eighties who resided in this nursing home. Edie was very intelligent and still quite influential in her community, regularly giving lectures and writing articles for local newspapers. As I passed by Edie's room this particular day, I noticed a framed letter of recognition mounted on her wall. I paused and asked her what it was for.

She explained it was in honor of the time and money she had donated in support of several causes such as the National Organization for Women and Planned Parenthood.

I carefully began questioning Edie regarding her views, and I told her about the work I did during the week for the Pregnancy Resource Centers. She was a highly educated and articulate person, and I felt a bit intimidated.

Edie asked me questions and expressed surprise when she learned that as early as five weeks following conception a baby's heart can be seen beating on the ultrasound screen; that at seven weeks following conception a baby can be seen twisting and moving about.

"If I were doing what you do, and seeing what you see, I just might change my opinions," Edie surprisingly responded. Then she quickly expressed her belief that it is the woman who must be considered first with pregnancy; that the woman should have the right to make the decision as to the outcome.

"What about the baby's rights?" I couldn't help asking.

Edie paused and then quietly replied, "I have to admit, I have never thought about that before." For her, it had always been about the woman.

Here was a bright, thoughtful woman, who for the majority of her adult years had championed women's rights, particularly a woman's reproductive rights. Yet she had honestly never thought about the baby!

Our hands instinctively clasped together and we sat there silently for a couple of minutes. Feeling it best not to press further, I told her I needed to get back to my duties and thanked her for taking the time to talk with me.

"Thank you, dear." Edie smiled sweetly and patted my arm.

As I walked out of her room, she said, "You have given me a lot to think about, but I am not going to change my mind."

I silently prayed that eventually she would change her mind; that somehow her firm resolve would be broken. Although Edie and I continued to have interesting conversations from time to time, the subject of abortion never arose between us again. I have no idea whether or not her views toward the unborn ever changed. But I do believe she was made to think.

Chapter Twenty-Two

IHAVE NEVER SOUGHT a divine revelation or experience. In Christ alone I have found truth, wholeness, and the peace that passes all human understanding. I am content knowing I am His child. Jesus is more than enough for me.

The times God has spoken to me in very distinct ways have occurred without any expectation or longing on my part. They just happened. But I am thankful for these experiences and consider them blessings. They serve to confirm and validate the work I am doing today.

When Satan bombards me with self-doubt, when discouragement sets in, when I begin to question my effectiveness for Jesus, or when I am tempted to quit, I reflect back on those times of revelation and find renewed confidence, knowing I am exactly where God has orchestrated me to be.

I find all of this incredibly sobering. My heart desires so desperately to live a life worthy of His calling. I fear I will be a hindrance in this process rather than an aid. I pray I will be unbending for Jesus and that His good purpose for my life will be realized. As the Psalmist aptly wrote: "Create in me a clean heart, O God; and renew a right spirit within me" (Psalm 51:10 NKJ). It is only by His grace.

A couple of years ago I had a vivid dream in which the rapture of the church was taking place. My senses were keenly aware of this blissful event. My spirit was elevated above my body, where I observed my face immersed in indescribable and absolute joy. A broad smile covered my face, creating a radiant glow. I was overcome with total, glorious euphoria.

I awoke to the sounds of dogs barking and a train whistle blowing, starkly reminding me that I was still on this earth. What a disappointment, realizing it had been only a dream! As I lay there praying, utterly consumed by this dream, Jesus impressed upon my heart that the time for His return is near. I must tell all those I can, especially the women I see at the Pregnancy Resource Centers, of the hope of eternal life in Him.

When I first became involved with the ministry of PRC, my heart burned with passion for the unborn. While that is still true today, God has given me an added passion for these babies' mothers. He has placed a real love for these ladies in my heart.

While the work that is being done through all of the pro-life ministries is wonderful, the most impacting effect it can have is if hearts are turned toward Jesus. What other motivation is there for a life-style change than one's love for Christ and the desire to honor Him? Even then it can still be so hard. Without Him, the likelihood of serious and lasting change is unlikely.

I awoke on one recent anniversary of Roe vs. Wade with a sick feeling, overtaken with sadness when I remembered what day it was. Sadness for the millions of babies whose lives have been taken; sadness in knowing my own baby is included in that number.

Once again, the enemy badgered me that this fight for life is unbeatable; that it is all too overwhelming. For a time that morning, I allowed myself to be drawn into his web of deceit.

Discouraged, I got out of bed, picked up my Bible, and walked to the sofa in our living room. I glanced out one of the large picture windows and caught sight of a rainbow, brilliantly displayed in the morning sky. It took me by surprise because the weather was not what would typically produce a rainbow. I hurried to the sliding door on the other side of the room to see if the rainbow was full. Sure enough, it was!

"*I am still in control. I have heard every cry. I have seen every tear,*" the Lord clearly spoke to my heart, impressing that He had not missed a thing.

When Jerry walked into the room, I eagerly told him all. Then looking out the same window, the rainbow was completely gone. Not a straggling hint of color left behind. It had not been more than ten minutes. I cannot say that God placed that rainbow in the sky that morning just for me, but I do believe He made sure I saw it.

Later that same morning I visited the Memorial for the Unborn in the Portland area. I do not go there often, but felt led to do so that day. Sitting on the small cement bench in front of the wall of names, I softly brushed my hand across my son's well-weathered plaque. Tears filled my eyes. The anniversary date of the legalization of abortion made this visit especially meaningful.

My tears were mainly for joy and gratitude, not only for the healing that God has brought to my own heart, but also for the hope and truth He has brought to thousands of women through ministries such as the Pregnancy Resource

Centers. I sat there in awe that He would choose me—such an unlikely prospect—to be a part of such a great work.

Chapter Twenty-Three

FOR A SHORT period of time, I was PRC's interim nurse manager. During this time, I experienced something I will never forget. One of my duties as nurse manager was to bring the ultrasound charts to PRC's doctors for review. When I arrived for the appointment I had arranged with one of the doctors, his nurse asked me to sit and wait in his office. The doctor was at the hospital next door, admitting a patient.

This particular patient had been referred to him by the Pregnancy Resource Centers. She had first come to PRC for a pregnancy test, which had read "positive." She then went to her own doctor, who diagnosed that her pregnancy was not progressing as it should. The doctor referred her to an abortion clinic, where she was told that having an abortion was harmless and all that was inside her was "just tissue, anyway."

Bewildered, and not wanting an abortion, this woman went back to PRC for counsel and support. She had been referred by PRC to the doctor now treating her. Upon initial examination and ultrasound, he determined the baby had died several weeks earlier. He administered a drug to cause her body to expel her baby naturally. She returned to his office the following morning—the morning I was there—with her baby. Her dead baby and part of the placenta were in a shopping bag. The nurse asked me if I wanted to see the baby.

What I observed was a perfectly formed, fifteen-week-old human being about five inches long. He had arms and legs, fingers and toes, two eyes, two ears, a nose, and a perfect little mouth. He was a baby, and far from being "just tissue, anyway."

About one month later I was sharing with an abortion-minded client that the following day would be thirty-one years since the abortion of my baby.

"And you still remember the date?" Mandy asked, sounding surprised.

"Yes, I remember everything about that day. I have found healing in Jesus, but my abortion still hurts."

"Do you need a hug?" she asked tenderly.

At first, not realizing her meaning, I said, "Do you need a hug?"

"No," she replied, "I think *you* need a hug."

"Sure," I answered.

We both stood, and Mandy hugged me tightly.

"Thank you. You are very sweet," I said.

I believe Jesus was giving me a hug that day and through a very unlikely source. On the surface, Mandy came across as hard and cold. Her mannerism was gruff. Her hair was greasy. There was dirt under her fingernails. Her body odor was hard to ignore. But when she hugged me, all I sensed was warmth and love.

After Mandy left the center, I thanked God for this encounter and prayed for the life of her baby. I also found myself praying that my grown son would call me the next day or, even better, that I would get to see him. It's not that he doesn't call or that I do not see him, but he is busy with his own life and family. I wouldn't necessarily have contact with him on that particular day. I felt a real need to hear from him on the anniversary of my other son's abortion.

When I got home from work that evening, I listened to a telephone message from my daughter-in-law, asking if my husband and I would be available to babysit our grandchildren the following evening—the anniversary of my abortion. Of course I told her we would! My son and daughter-in-law stayed for a couple of hours after returning to pick up their children that following evening. Just hearing my son's voice and having him in our home on that poignant date ministered immensely to me.

There are prayers that never seem to get answered exactly as I hope, and others that are answered beyond my expectations. Yet, whether they are answered as I hoped or not, I have learned that I must trust Him. I know that in regards to His children, God brings all things to a good end, but how often I need reminding!

When Mandy had left the center after our hug, she was still expressing her intent to abort. Two weeks later she returned, still pregnant, and said she had not yet made up her mind.

I was sitting at my desk in the ultrasound room eleven months later when Mandy poked her head into the room. "Hi, do you remember me? I had my baby. Having my son is the best choice I ever made. Thank you for understanding what I was going through."

After she left, I had my own mini-praise session with God. I marveled at how much He cares, not only for Mandy and her baby boy, but also for me. He cared enough to arrange for Mandy to pass by the ultrasound room on a day I was there and not busy with another client, and then had her take the time to stop and talk to me. This absolutely blows me away! And the fact that she made the choice to give birth to her son and is so thankful for having done so …? Well, what can I say? That alone overwhelms my soul. God is a most awesome God!

I will always remember Mandy and the kindness she showed me. I have had clients hug me out of gratitude, but she is the only one who has done so in an attempt to bring me comfort.

Chapter Twenty-Four

I HAD BEEN AN ultrasound nurse for PRC for four years and had grown quite content when, once again, I was stretched out of my comfort zone. I was offered the position of director as well as nurse for an entirely *different* center. There are five centers in the greater Portland area.

It was hard to leave what I knew and the volunteers and staff I had grown comfortable with. Becoming a director was not something I had considered or would have sought on my own. The transition went smoothly, however. The difficulties I had anticipated were all but non-existent. Yet after a short season, I began to feel unsettled. Being Center Director consumed the bulk of my time and focus, while the ultrasound portion—to which I felt so strongly called—became a poor second. After nine months of being the director, I returned to the sole position of ultrasound nurse for PRC.

Several years after that, and after six years of the Pregnancy Resource Centers being my sole employment, God shifted my life … again. I began to have thoughts of leaving PRC altogether. Initially, I dismissed these thoughts as quickly as they entered my mind. *Where in the world did that come from?* I responded almost angrily. From the time I was hired by PRC, I had never given any serious thought to leaving. I loved being part of the ministry of PRC and was as happy as could be serving there. For one full year I struggled with wondering if maybe my time with PRC was up.

From the beginning I had known I would be with PRC for only as long as God wanted me there. When He told me it was time to go, I would leave. But when I actually began to sense it was time to leave, I found it extremely difficult. God had called me to PRC in the first place. I couldn't leave until I was positive *He* was calling me away.

During that year I earnestly sought God for direction and clarity, prostrating myself before Him in heart-wrenching prayer and with fasting. Then one Friday afternoon I suddenly became overwhelmed with the understanding that it was time for me to leave.

"Just like that? Without any warning?" I implored.

"*One year is not time enough? Go,*" I sensed God speaking.

"But, Lord!"

"*Go.*"

"Okay," I numbly answered.

I felt as though my heart would break. That weekend was very long for me. I could think of nothing else. Yet at the same time, I had such peace. I had total confidence that God was leading me, which made it all okay. What took priority for me was the desire to be in the center of God's will. I had no choice than to do what He was telling me to do. I had to leave! I prayed all weekend that God would be with me when I told Nancy, PRC's Nurse Manager.

When I telephoned Nancy that Monday morning, I had initially intended to ask her if we could meet someplace to talk. I had not planned to tell her over the phone that I was leaving. But when I heard her sweet, gentle voice, I lost it. I sat at my desk in the ultrasound room and sobbed, attempting to converse coherently.

Nancy asked me to think about and pray over my decision for one full week before making it final. She asked if we could talk again the following Monday, which would be exactly one week. I agreed to her request.

Over the course of the previous year I had been thinking about the Jewish nursing home where I had once been employed. I believed God was leading me back there. Before my telephone call to Nancy, I had made contact with the Director of Nurses at the nursing home. She informed me that the only nursing position currently available was an on-call one.

Toward the end of that week I knew unquestionably that I was to leave PRC, but I also began to believe that my time away from PRC would not be permanent.

Nikki, the director of the PRC center I was then working at told me, "Missionaries take furloughs to rest. Maybe this is just a time of rest for you."

Several others told me the same thing. Also toward the end of the week of my agreement with Nancy, I was offered a full-time position with the Jewish nursing home. I felt a strong hesitancy in my spirit. *Don't get yourself locked in there. Don't get yourself locked in there,* kept rolling around in my head.

I told the Director of Nurses that I would most likely accept the on-call position, but I would think about her full-time offer and let her know. She told me what my hourly rate would be. Whew! Once I was back in my car, I grabbed my calculator and did some quick number crunching. It was tempting! The pay was a lot more money than what I had been earning with PRC.

Still, I felt a firm check in my spirit. *Don't get yourself locked in there. Don't get yourself locked in there.*

Over the weekend, I continued to seek God, but my prayer changed. I knew He was calling me away from PRC for what I believed to be a season of rest. I needed to know for sure, though. I did not want to let my emotions lead. I wanted God to have total control of the reins. *My desires or feelings were not important.*

By Sunday morning I was tired. Tired of talking, tired of praying, and tired of crying. I had done a lot of explaining and a lot of crying that week. I was tired—just plain tired. I did not want to go to church. I did not want to see anyone that day. I did not want to talk to anyone that day. And I was not in the mood for the relatives we had already invited to our home for lunch that day.

"I'm tired, and I am not in the mood for church or for company today. I am not in the mood for *anything*," I whined to Jerry. He just hugged me. He was so supportive through all of this.

Well ... I knew I needed to go to church, and I couldn't cancel the relatives. But I decided I would avoid talking to anyone at church. We would just slip in and out. I would just have to put on my best front and get through the day.

I had prayed to God earlier that morning, telling Him I needed to know *today* what to tell Nancy. I had already concluded I would tell her I was only leaving PRC for a season—for six months—for a time of rest. But I needed clear confirmation from God. I needed to know *for sure* if this was what He wanted, or if it was just me. As sad as it would be to leave PRC for good, I would be okay with it as long as I *truly believed* it was what God desired. I prayed:

"I need to know today, Lord. I need to know if You are calling me away from PRC for good or only for a time. I believe you are calling me away from PRC temporarily, for a season of rest, for six months. I believe this is what I am to tell Nancy. But I need to know for sure, before I talk to Nancy tomorrow morning. I need to know *today*, Lord, if I am making the right decision."

We arrived at church, and Jerry stopped and talked with somebody. I hurried upstairs and sat in the back row, in the farthest corner, avoiding our usual spots, which are more conspicuous. I pretended to read the bulletin, relieved I would not have to talk to anyone.

Then here came Rachel! Not only did she stop directly in front of me, but she knelt on the floor in front of me and looked directly into my eyes. "Could you use a break from having home group at your house for a while? We all need a break now and then. I feel like you could use some rest."

I nodded, and tears filled my eyes.

After Rachel walked away, somebody else "found" me. She was a lady I had spoken with just one other time, a month or so earlier. I was not even sure of her name. I'm still not sure. She smiled at me. "Hi, how are you doing? I've been thinking about you all week."

That's weird, I thought to myself. *You don't even know me. We only talked once.* "What have you been thinking about me?" I smiled politely.

"Oh, nothing really. You've just been on my heart. I've been praying for you. You're tired, aren't you?"

I was speechless.

The worship time began, and my awareness of the presence of the Holy Spirit was overwhelming. Tears flowed down my face. "Oh Lord, you are so good to me," I cried.

It seemed like God was speaking to me through the sermon, as well. The pastor talked about the battles we all face. Sometimes God removes us from the "lions' den" for a time of rest, but then He puts us back in the battle again. He talked about the importance of being in the center of

God's will. It is not about driving a fancy car or about having a nice house or a big, fat bank account ... *hmmm* ... but about being exactly where God has placed you, and resting in Him.

At those words, Rachel's head turned sharply in my direction, and our eyes met.

Following the service, I told Jerry I needed to ask Rachel why she had turned her head to look at me.

"That was for you," Rachel smiled. "You are making the right decision. You can rest in God that you are in the center of His will."

That was it. I now had no doubt God was calling me away from PRC for a season of rest, and that I would be returning. I felt confident that I was not to take the full-time position at the nursing home, either. I was not to *get myself locked in there*. Rather, I would take the on-call position and be ready to return to PRC, which I believed would be in six months.

My season of rest was good. I spent a lot more time just staying at home, and more time with family and friends. I enjoyed being a floor nurse again. It was a complete contrast from PRC, and it was good for me to have that time away. It was definitely an emotional season of rest. I had not realized how tired I had become.

God clearly confirmed to me that I would return to PRC in six months, which I have recently done. I look forward to this new season and to all that God has in store.

I have returned to PRC with the heightened awareness that I am only here by His call, and only until He again calls me away. None of this has anything to do with me but everything to do with Him.

I believe He uses each of us at different times and in different ways. There are many worthy venues for serving

Him. The important thing is to be obedient—no matter how or where He leads, and for however *long* He leads.

I am continually in awe at His sovereignty and faithfulness in leading and equipping me. I know that in and of myself I am so very inadequate.

> "So neither he who plants nor he who waters is anything; but only God, who makes things grow."
> —1 Corinthians 3:7

Conclusion

IHAVE KNOWN THE loneliness of walking apart from God, the futility of doing things my own way and seeking the desires of my own selfish will. I have experienced the pain of separation from Him, due to the wall my sin has erected—thinking I knew a better path than the one my Lord had carefully laid out before my mother felt the first pangs of my birth. I have fought and strived to do it on my own, and I fall flat on my face every time. I'm left lying empty and sad.

I also know the joy and total peace of a submitted and willing heart. I know the inner satisfaction and rest of holding firmly to Him.

Today, I cannot imagine walking anywhere else than beneath the safety of God's grace and covering. To lose the joy of abiding in Him is not a choice I am willing to make. I have been there, and I have learned it is not worth the cost.

"I remember my affliction and my wandering, the bitterness and the gall. I well remember them. Yet this I call to mind and therefore I have hope; because of the Lord's great love we are not consumed, for his compassions never fail. They are new every morning; great is Your faithfulness. I say to myself, The Lord is my portion; therefore I will wait for him. The Lord is good to those whose hope is in him, to the one who seeks him; it is good to wait quietly for the salvation of the Lord" (Lamentations 3:19-26).

To my wonderful, merciful Savior, the joy of my heart and the lifter of my head, I pledge my allegiance. In Him alone do I place my trust.

I've prayed throughout the process of writing this book that God's grace would abound. He alone is deserving of all the glory, honor, and praise.

I praise God for healing me and setting me free from the bondage of my abortion. Without His healing I would not be able to do the work I am doing today. There is no way I could look at those sweet babies on the ultrasound screen if my Savior had not looked upon me with His eyes of mercy and if He had not immersed me in His healing balm of love.

I am thrilled that God has chosen to use me in the way He has ... in a "Ministry for Grieving Women."

There are still moments that bring a sudden twinge of real sadness, regret, and even guilt over the abortion of my baby. A part of me will always feel the loss of my son. I am sure this will be the case until I am with Jesus. God promises to forget the sins of those who call upon the name of his Son, Jesus. As human beings, we are not so capable of forgetting.

Until we are given our new, eternal bodies and minds, life will be a struggle. I often wonder how people who do not have Jesus make sense of it all. How do they deal with the heartaches and the pressures of this weary old world? I cannot imagine where I would be without my Lord.

I am thankful that those moments of sadness and regret are just twinges, replaced as quickly as they come by a sense of peace and joy. Peace from knowing I am whole and righteous in my Savior's eyes, and in knowing my baby is safe and content in the arms of my wonderful Lord. And inexpressible joy from knowing and loving Jesus.

This past Christmas Eve I sat in church, gazing at the prettily decorated Christmas tree and singing "Silent Night." I suddenly became overwhelmed with the awareness that God was in this place and that He loves me very much. It was as if, for the very first time, I fully comprehended the depth of His love for me. From as far back as I can remember I have known God loves me. But that night I realized more than ever how personal His love for me is. That He intensely loves *me*, Gayle.

What made this all the more moving was that we were visiting my husband's parents for Christmas and attending their church for Christmas Eve. Their church (by my definition) is very dry and somber. I went to church that night not expecting to receive much. I left with a Christmas gift I will carry with me always. Knowing how much He loves me and knowing He does all for my good enables me to trust Him all the more.

If anyone reading this is hurting from a past abortion, please know how very wide and long and high and deep the love of God is for you. His arms are strong and capable and more than willing to embrace and heal you. Listen carefully, look boldly into His Holy Word, and you will hear Him softly calling:

"Come to Me, all who are weary and heavy laden, and I will give you rest."
—Matthew 11:28 (NASB)

And:

"For I know the plans I have for you, declares the Lord, plans to prosper you and not to harm you, plans to give you hope and a future."
—Jeremiah 29:11

Sources

B ROCHURES, ARTICLES, AND books I found useful while writing this story:

Brind, J., et al. "Induced Abortion As an Independent Risk Factor for Breast Cancer: A Comprehensive Review and Meta-analysis." Hershey Medical Center, 1996.

Garfinkel, et al. "Stress, Depression, and Suicide: A Study of Adolescents in Minnesota." Minneapolis, MN. University of Minnesota Extension Service, 1986.

Jones RK, Darroch JE, Henshaw SK. *Perspectives on Sexual and Reproductive Health.* 2002.

Reardon, David C. "A Survey of Psychological Reactions." Springfield, IL. Elliot Institute, 1987.

"Making an Informed Decision about Your Pregnancy." Grand Rapids, MI. Frontlines Publishing.

David C. Reardon, "Aborted Women-Silent No More."

"Abortion Raises Breast Cancer Risk" brochure; Coalition on Abortion / Breast Cancer, An International Women's Association.

"What They Never Told You About the Facts of Life" brochure; Human Development Resource Council, Inc.

"The First Nine Months" Brochure; Focus on the Family Publishing.

Helen Harrison, "*The Premature Baby Book.*"

Study by the Center for Reason (prweb.com).

"Christians Have as Many Abortions as Everyone Else, Catholics Have More"; Compiled & Edited, Edward T. Babinski.

Jones RK, Darroch JE, Henshaw SK, Patterns in the Socioeconomic, characteristics of women obtaining abortions in 2000-2001. *Perspectives on Sexual and Reproductive Health*, 2002.

All scripture passages are taken from the King James, New King James, New International, or New American Standard Versions of the Bible.

PW

To order additional copies of this book call:
1-877-421-READ (7323)
or please visit our Web site at
www.pleasantwordbooks.com

If you enjoyed this quality custom-published book,
drop by our Web site for more books and information.

www.winepressgroup.com
"Your partner in custom publishing."